# Resume Psychology©

## Resume Hacks & Traps Revealed
## Beat the Machine. Be Seen. Get Hired!

Dirk Spencer

# Resume Psychology

Table of Contents

## Introduction

*Back in the day* as a Computer Specialist, General Schedule 12 (GS12) Series 334 (which no longer exists), my job was writing program code for mainframe computers and eventually migrating to office automation (personal computers), developing and delivering technical training, creation of technical proposals, design, test and installation of local area networks, and work on a robotic inventory systems used for aviation aircraft repair and maintenance. There was an abundance of computer vendor training, testing across various and proprietary computer platforms which was all put to good use. These varied experiences gave me a great foundation on how computers process information, execute program logic, and read and write data to storage. This provided me with a bit by bit, byte by byte understanding of how computer memory, storage and processors were logically and physically manipulated to full-fill all the activities performed by the software and hardware components.

Fast forward to when people began to access the Internet through their cable providers instead of their landlines. Here is when people seemed to need help understanding the new era of job search. Things like the Internet and World Wide Web changed how people applied for jobs. This is when I started doing resume and job board presentations based on my technical experience.

## From Computer Specialist to Resume Psychologist

While in my car the cell phone rang.

A recruiter friend was on the line and said, *"Dirk, a mutual friend of ours needs to sort out his resume. You live only a block away from him. Could you stop by his place and give him some help?"*

She explained she had a customer who needed someone with our friend's talent base, but given the current state of his resume he would not be taken seriously by the client.

Because I am socially clumsy, awkward, and shy, my initial reaction was to turn the car away from my friend's house, so I could claim I was not nearby. But when I looked to my left and to my right the traffic was so bad there was nowhere to go. If I turned one way, I would be stuck in a line of cars waiting at a coffee shop grand opening. If I turned the other way, I would wind up in the parking lot of a national retail chain also having a grand opening. The intersection was clogged with cars trying to turn or U-turn. This was not my finest hour putting this much effort and thought to avoid this request without having to lie. Eventually, though, despite all of my attempts to subvert traffic and go in the complete opposite direction, I ended up stopped in the left-hand turn lane to pull into my friend's cul-de-sac.

I sucked it up and made the turn.

"Come on in, come on in," my friend said at the door. I followed him down the hallway the whole while awkwardly fending off his beloved dog. This sweet-beast of a pet tried to stick his snout in the various crevices associated with my pants (thank God I was not wearing shorts).

We finally made it to the office, which was beautifully decorated because our friend's wife was an interior designer.

Tucked inside an antique armoire was the computer. It was one of the original IBM® personal computers with the infamous green cathode ray tube (CRT) monitor, the click-clack keyboard, and an Okidata® pinhead dot matrix printer.

Now, our friend was the quintessential, ruggedly handsome guy. He was 6'5". In a suit, he looked like he should be in the black and white episodes of Bewitched as one of Tate's bosses. At 5'10" and not so handsome, myself, it was easy to be envious of his looks, his advanced education, excellent certifications, and illustrious career. He was also a very likable guy so it was easy to become his friend.

Why go through all this with you here? It is important for you to understand the situation. This was a guy who had it all going for him. There was no doubt he knew how to do the job. The only reason he was unemployed was because the company he worked for had European ownership.

When the market went down, instead of laying off people in Europe, they laid them off in the US. It was cheaper for them to do so given termination, reduction in force and severance legislation overseas.

Yes, it may seem a little silly to go on and on about this guy, but it is important to have this imagery in your head of the kind of person he was. It is important to appreciate the frustration he was feeling through no fault of his own.

With the computer booted up, he hands me a copy of the email from the recruiter with the job description on it. I read it aloud to force myself to focus.

"Okay," I nodded. "Now, show me where your resume describes this type of work experience."

He pointed to a paragraph on the computer's monitor.

I read what he indicated and thought, "*Maybe I have put too much faith in this guy's appearance and what he says he has done.*"

At the risk of our friendship, I finally asked the hard question: "*Do you have this experience in your career background somewhere?*"

He looked at me with a very direct gaze and with supreme confidence said, "*Like I said, it's in there.*"

The problem was the words in the email were not in the section of the resume he had me read. None. Not a single matching word.

I ask another question, "*Where else do you have this experience?*"

He pointed to two or three more sections of his resume.

But again, the words on the email did not appear in those sections of his resume either.

To say I was confused would be an understatement. And only because I had come to know this man as a friend did I hang through the process. I knew I needed to figure out what was missing, to find the delta between his stories, his career experience, and how it was presented to the world through his resume.

His networking conversations were filled with technical jargon, using keywords on process control and budgetary data only someone in his position would be able to access and share so fluidly. Every time he talked about his profession, I found myself wanting to change careers. I found myself wanting to follow him on his next project.

But his resume? Oh my God. It was like the resume hid his experience deliberately.

The content on the resume was unbelievably vague. It made me question whether or not he actually had the experience. This was a dangerous resume.

Technically, we had enough time to replace a vague word used repeatedly in the resume with a less-vague word or less-vague phrase. The goal was to provide better detail. It had to match the job description in the email. He had to express the correct experience in the resume.

Given the time constraints by the recruiter we modified a vague word by using a *less* vague word or a *less* vague phrase in its place. That was the fix.

Twenty minutes later we emailed the updated resume to the recruiter.

About an hour later our friend had an in-person interview.

By sundown, he had an offer!

What made these results so impressive was our friend had been on the bench for nearly 2 years with no legitimate offers.

The bigger surprise to this story?

My friend turned the company down! He did not accept the job.

Why?

He now had a resume which generated offers!

## Resume Psychology (RP) is Born

The experience of helping a friend land a job-offer made an impression.

It seemed it would be possible to create a repeatable process.

A process anyone from blue-collar to white-collar could follow to create better resumes to increase the likelihood of more job offers. This idea of putting the power of creating an impactful resume back with the individual was the moment Resume Psychology (RP) was born.

The question was: How to create a repeatable resume-creation process?

The answer would require deliberate research on recruiter

technology, resume automation, business unit organization,

and ranking strategies.

It started with exploring and researching collateral topics such

as:

- Boolean search engines
- Boolean logic operators
- Database query methods
- Applicant tracking software
- Vendor management systems
- Artificial intelligence modules
- Fuzzy logic machines
- Algorithms
- Eye-movement patterns
- Linguistics
- Structured Query Language (SQL)
- Keyword ranking strategies

While reviewing the research options it was obvious there

would be a need to:

- Ignore the conventional wisdom of corporate outplacement
  firms
- Stop taking advice from staffing executives 20 years
  removed from the Internet
- Discontinue accepting resume writer's advice who are
  certified by an email-quiz
- Ignore advice from people with PhDs in English and
  Literature
- Disregard executive search advice telling candidates to
  keep their resumes off-line

It might seem harsh deciding all of these *other* people were

wrong. But it was obvious people in search-mode, seeking

employment needed straight-talk or more current information to help them to be more competitive in an automated job market. To avoid adopting out-of-date information or practices it would be important to use:

- Peer-reviewed source material only
- Direct interviews with industry experts on recruiting technology, processes, and behaviors
- Empirical examples
- Resume vendor data

"Peer-reviewed" materials mean experts have evaluated the content of other experts from the same field. These sources come from scientific, academic and similar professions. It is a form of review rigor not used in most of the resume advice posted online or given by resume writers or outplacement firms. When possible, I interviewed sources directly. This included every phone call with a recruiter or HR person. It was very simple to ask questions and drill down on their experience as if it was an interview for an industry magazine. This was also done with vendor reps, as well as their customer support people (by complaining loud and clear whenever possible as a recruiter).

Then there were empirical examples used to explain documented or observed outcomes. This means before recommending a tactic on the resume, it had to have a large data set supporting a useable outcome for the resume. Additional research was done on linguistics, too. The concept that words have an impact beyond their definition. Written statements have an emotive effect and could potentially be leveraged to convey experiences on the resume.

In full disclosure, I tested fake resumes on job boards. The vendors and the customers with open jobs *frown* upon fake profiles a great deal even for test purposes. I *do not* recommend this strategy to anyone. My fake profiles with fake resumes tested genders, keywords, and job titles. I used fictitious names for positions in which I had no expertise. Using the right keywords worked over and over again based on the number of follow-up calls received.

Lastly, transitioning to my new career as a recruiter along with my previous experience with computer software and hardware would allow me to ask very specific questions of ATS (Applicant Tracking System), VMS (Vendor Management Systems) and multiple job board vendors. These efforts resulted in multiple invitations to work on beta-test teams for new releases. The beta-tests included using new resume or candidate sorting and ranking features, writing reviews, and providing outcome reports to my management. This happened twice at two different companies. In one instance I submitted so many error reports about features not working the account manager gave me direct access to his development team.

## What is Resume Psychology?

Resume Psychology (RP) is a fact based approach to developing resume content. This means Resume Psychology (RP) is focused on what can be verified and measured around resume content, layout and ranking. The goal is to have a repeatable process anyone can follow. It is not based on resume traditions unless required for a people, process or technology hack.

In Resume Psychology (RP) we bypass advice from those lacking professional recruiting experience. Professional experience requires high-volume recruiting using high-end automated resume and candidate management technology with audited government compliance requirements.

Resume Psychology (RP) allows us to hack the machine, be seen, and get hired. We do this by leveraging insights into:

- Organizational and human behavior

- Changes in job board search and resume collection
- Applicant tracking system (ATS) technology advancements
- Changes to recruiting processes and controls
- Process failure points with manual resume handling
- Company strategies to mitigate compliance risks
- Fear-based decision making
- Government audits for regulatory compliance
- Keyword strategies necessary with new technology
- Implementing inefficient writing to enable efficient reading
- Avoiding the "Kiss of Death" words and phrases

Resume Psychology (RP) should lead to more job offers using the hacks (and avoiding the traps) shared in this book. It should position candidates ahead of their competition. The outcome should lead to the resume being seen more frequently by the human reading using job boards or application tracking systems (ATS). In turn this should produce more phone screens and interviews, both of which should lead to more job offers.

**What You Need to Know About Your Resume**

A lot of resume writers and outplacement firms routinely preach that a resume is a marketing document. They are wrong.

Your resume is far more important!

Your resume is an anthropological documentation of your career. You will use it to land your next great opportunity.

Thinking of the resume as anything less leads you to shortchanging yourself and short-circuiting your chances to receive more job offers.

**What do resumes and lasers have in common?**

To be effective, they both have to be tightly focused on a single point.

For the laser, all of its energy is focused on a single point in space. Whether it's a laser site scope targeting game in the wild or a laser guided missile system, all the energy from the laser is focused to one solitary point.

With the resume it must be focused on one congruent topic (a set of work experiences) in order to land an interview.

Preferably a job-offer!

**The 3-Rs of Resumes**

The resume is a game of three distinct items: reachability, readability, and relatability.

Reachability may sound obvious and simple, but on a regular basis people submit their resume without their name, without their phone number, and most regrettably, without their email address. No one is using the US Postal Service to reach candidates in the age of the Internet. Most recruiters are not going to spend the time to research how to contact a job candidate if the information is missing. If the contact information is not easy to come by on a resume, the recruiter is simply going to move on to the next candidate.

Resume readability is all about structure. A resume should have easy to read content, a consistent layout, and simple formatting. Photographs, graphics, and fancy word processing tactics are distracting. Sometimes the best-qualified candidates have the most difficult resumes to read because they use the resume to show off their word processing chops, rather than to communicate their skills effectively.

Relatability is all about how a candidate presents their experience. Is the presentation too formal, too stiff, or too vague? The most qualified candidates do not automatically receive interviews. It is the candidate who finds a balance to their presentation on the resume and can bypass the traps associated with resume automation.

## What is Your Goal?

The goal should be to land a job, right?

This means you want to create a resume far and above the norm.

During my presentation series I would ask this question: "Who wants an interview?" The hands would go up in the air automatically.

Then I would ask this question: "Who wants a job offer"?

You could see the confusion in the faces of the attendees. You could see the confusion in how their hands would flex up and down not knowing which outcome was better.

Your goal with the resume should be to attract *offers* instead of interviews! This line of thinking does not sit well with everyone. There are recruiters who have said: "*Dirk that is crazy. I have never hired a candidate solely because of his resume.*" And my response has been: "*Maybe that's because no one has written a resume to that level.*"

Obviously this means *my bias* has taken over. But there had to be a better way for people to compete through their resume. Which begs the question: how can you combine reachability, readability, and relatability strategies to make your resume work for you? How can you write a resume strong enough to garner jobs rather than interviews? This is where Resume Psychology (RP) comes into play.

## LCD: A Resume Psychology Construct

Perhaps the primary driver in developing the Resume Psychology (RP) principles is the idea of the Lowest Common Denominator (LCD).

To ensure Resume Psychology (RP) worked across multiple areas, the techniques had to accommodate the lowest common denominator for each scenario a resume would be exposed. This strategy produces a core set of rules which we will review throughout the book.

While the application of the LCD is not very exciting it has a great deal of impact on how people should approach resume development.

## An Important Note about Recruiting

Recruiting is a unique position in any company. Some view it as a utility item to be turned on or off as needed. Other firms view it as a vital component to the human resources department. No matter how recruiting is managed there are 3 things impacting the resume: processes, people, and technology. Many of the processes in place are a response to regulations from both the state and federal governments which affect the resume. Each company will make an effort, in some fashion, to standardize the process of resume collection, storage, and review.

Companies of the same relative-size operate under the same pressures with and without resume-related technology.

Many do it with and without legal counsel to interpret resume-related regulations. This is why there is no single best-way or standard on these issues.

The technology is built to hit a sweet spot which balances government compliance, mitigates risk for a price-point which attracts enough customers to keep them in business. Realize companies using the same vendors may have totally different solutions in place.

Hiring people happens inside and outside "the lines" drawn by these differences. Usually there is no one-way of compensating for the variations in process failure, people behavior and quirks in the technology. Naturally, changes in leadership, vendor or budget can level significant changes without a change control process in sight. Again this is why it seems different every time a resume is submitted by the candidate.

No matter the people or the processes, resumes will typically be managed and filtered through the applicant tracking software (ATS) at your target company.

This could be a spreadsheet. It could be a job board costing them tens of thousands of dollars every year.

This technology used to be the domain of large corporations exclusively. Large companies were the only ones who needed and could afford software to manage the recruiting process. Today, no matter the size of the business, modern resumes are nearly always managed through some sort of computer software or application. Applicant tracking systems (ATS) have become relatively inexpensive to buy (or rent). Companies take on these costs to help demonstrate their commitment to regulatory compliance if not augment recruiting staff. These systems are a form of insurance in some cases and in others necessary given the volume of resumes received.

The vendors in the ATS business have a goal of making money. Usually, the software is offered on a tiered pricing plan, with more features being offered without increasing the cost automatically. Consequently, while an ATS may offer solutions for two or three very specific pain points in the hiring process, many companies do not use products offering total solutions. Resume Psychology (RP) was developed with some overarching strategies to produce a better document and to help the resume conform to potential ATS software issues; hence the need for an LCD.

**How I Know Resume Psychology Works**

First and foremost, the information is specialized. There is no way to know these things without research and computer software experience or paying for these services which can be hundreds of thousands a year for large firms seeking turn-key solutions.

On a personal level you know you have arrived when people call you because *others* invoke *your name* when questioning *their* training. And, it's even more official when swearing is involved!

After doing Resume Psychology (RP) presentations locally, for the better part of a year, I received a vague voicemail from an outplacement firm requesting a callback.

Dialing the number back, I was put on hold for the briefest of moments. When the hold music dropped off a voice asked:

"Who the f*#k are you?"

No joke. True story.

Once I stopped laughing, I blurted out, "Excuse me?"

"I know who you are," was the reply. This individual proceeded to outline why she called. It seems their resume audience members would correct their instructors on resume methods during their classes or workshops. The audience members were interrupting the trainers repeatedly during these sessions. Inevitably the audience members would start a statement with: "*Well, Dirk said...*" hence the "*who is Dirk?*" call.

In my mind, it was obvious their presenters were not trained on how to handle contrary suggestions working from scripted content. These people were typically contractors who most likely believed they were walking into a straight-up presentation situation – not a debate class.

There had been stories about full-on *arguments* at some of these events. My thought was exuberance among job-seekers was the issue. I had no idea these debates were disrupting the conventional wisdom to the degree it warranted a phone call to determine my place in the resume arena.

Moving forward on the call, we discussed at a high-level what the Resume Psychology (RP) approach was in general. We talked about the biases of the people, process issues and the technology.

"Well, we don't do that here," was the response and the call was over.

This call told me RP had hit critical mass. If people were questioning resume help bought and paid for by their previous company, it was possible they were receiving more out of their outplacement dollars. It also meant RP was making an impact. Since then, many of the local outplacement firms have hired recruiters who use RP to help their clients. This started with a checklist I created and used at public events along with templates and content creation lectures.

My attorney tells me he can issue cease and desist orders to people and organizations using my content without having paid a royalty. But the goal of RP is to help people and not incite legal drama.

Maybe the better way to put this is say the goal is to put the

power back in the hands of the people seeking employment?

Hopeful more people find their next job sooner than later

applying the guidelines in Resume Psychology (RP).

**How to Use this Book**

Here are a few suggestions on ways to use the material:

1. Learn what it takes to create a competitive resume for technology based hiring
2. Perform quality checks on resume material created by a third-party on your behalf
3. Collaborate with your resume writer using this book as your guide
4. Use this book to teach others how technology affects resumes and hiring
5. Use this book to start a career transition ministry near you
6. Have a resume party and divide and conquer the book content against your needs
7. Hire a career coach and have them work with you implementing these strategies
8. Google pro bono resources and enlist their assistance to help you use the book

This book is organized around the 4-Cs, which are the core

concepts of Resume Psychology (RP).

**At a glance - The 4-Cs are:**

- Content
- Context
- Clarity
- Consistency

The 4-Cs method is a way for people to deconstruct and reassemble the industry jargon, professional experience, career scale, and job stability as related by the resume.

**Content – The First C**

Perfecting resume content is a tricky endeavor. There is a lot of advice centered on the idea of the resume as a marketing document. Obviously, my bias is against this advice. With the arrival of new recruiter technology and processes, such advice is dated.

In my mind, the resume is an anthropological story of your career experience. It is serious business, and it is vitally important you understand what constitutes great resume content. Great content speaks to a level of specifics, details, and examples allowing the hiring manager enough confidence to risk an offer or at a minimum an interview.

**Resume Formats**

**Reverse Chronological Resume**

When developing a resume, you want to use what we call in the industry a "reverse chronological" resume. In simplest terms, a reverse chronological resume means you start with your most recent job position and work backwards job to job. The goal is to outline your workplaces, job titles, dates of employment, and listing of your experiences.

Essentially you are working backwards from now through your past.

The reverse chronological resume is a tradition which will probably be around for a long time to come.

Why?

Because the ATS technology reinforces its continued use. The reverse chronological resume format is the database record layout used by virtually all ATS and VMS (vendor management software) product providers. Which is to say, the ATS and VMS software companies assume the data on the resume will be presented in reverse chronological order.

Plus, the reverse chronological resume is expected by hiring managers.

**The Functional Resume**

The functional resume is usually recommended for individuals reentering the workforce after an absence or work-at-home spouses starting a career. Often these are people who took time off a career, worked from home, or relocated frequently due to a spouse's job change. Their work history may seem choppy and show multiple employment gaps if they worked outside the home.

The goal of the functional resume is to showcase talents and skills without telegraphing when those skills were acquired and subsequently applied.

Hiring managers, HR professionals, and recruiters are generally less accepting of the functional resume. By its very design and layout, the functional resume draws attention to the lack of specificity regarding times and dates.

The functional resume is also typically difficult to translate into any ATS. Usually, the bare minimum of information is loaded since there is no logical or physical placeholder for the "guts" of the functional resume where the experience is listed. This is due to the technology not being developed for this data-layout. When the functional resume is pulled up electronically, the recruiter or the hiring manager will see a list of companies and job titles (if present) with no supporting experience statements. This makes the resume look incomplete and unprofessional. Candidates using the functional resume will likely not receive calls, let alone interviews, unless they meet very specific or unique skills required by the company.

The bottom line is, thanks to the ATS software limitations submitting functional resumes creates more questions than answers. The best time to use a functional resume is when you have personal access to the hiring manager or recruiter at a job fair or networking event.

## The Hybrid Resume

The hybrid resume attempts to combine the best features of a reverse chronological resume and the best features of a functional resume. It is an attempt to give a narrative on overall skills, regardless of when they were used and to show job experiences with specific times and dates for when the skills or knowledge was acquired.

The hybrid resume has the same technical issues as the functional resume; there's a limit on how or if the information is stored digitally.

In rare cases where the narrative (job experiences not listed by company) is captured by the ATS because it's not assigned, categorized, or organized under a specific job, company, or title, the hiring manager and the recruiter will largely ignore the information.

Lastly, there is no movement or demand by the recruiting industry requesting or even requiring the ATS vendors to develop solutions which would allow for the effective collection of information from a functional or hybrid resume. This is why these formats *should not be* considered as an option for your resume if at all possible.

**Physical Layout**

Given what we know about how ATS technology processes data, it is vital to consider some fundamental rules about resume layout.

We will go into more detail in subsequent sections but for now use this list as a reference:

- Introductory paragraph – limit to three lines max
- Bullets – use conventional dots or dashes only
- Margins – use 1-inch margins on all four sides of the page
- Ragged right – use left-justified text for work experience sections forward on the resume
- Section labels – such as "Summary" "Overview" "Preview" "Professional Experience" *can* be preceded by the current job title or keyword to increase the keyword hit rate

**Paragraphs**

The introductory paragraph exists to help the recruiter or hiring manager present your skills to those who will be doing the interview. It saves the recruiter time no doubt and helps him or her understand where you fit within their organization. And while I rail against traditional resume advice, this falls under a people behavior hack we wish to leverage.

The other goal of the intro paragraph is to be keyword-rich and easy to understand. It should convey a certain level of skill and portray you with a certain level of confidence when the wording may appear abstract.

**Intro Paragraph Template:**

- "Job title" with expertise in <keyword skill 1>, <keyword skill 2>, and <keyword skill 3> with <keyword skill 4>, <keyword skill 5>, and <keyword skill 6> with <industry name 1>, <industry name 2>, and <industry name 3>.

**Examples - Intro Paragraphs:**

- Graphic designer with expertise in visual layout, color mixing, and line drawing using Adobe Suite, CorelDraw, and Camtasia with fashion design, Photoshop projects, and content curation for consistent branding across all channels.

- Project manager with expertise in Kanban, Scrum, and Agile project methodologies using MS Project and proprietary software in highway construction, office-park builds, and telecommunications infrastructures for defense and municipalities.

- Business analyst with expertise in SWOT and root-cause analysis, along with survey and requirement elicitation, as a liaison between technical teams and management to verify technical specifications and user-adoption of application systems.

**Bullets**

It is best to avoid specialty bullets. This is an LCD criterion.

Why?

Using graphic icons or special characters as bullets can cause your text data to be deleted in ATS. There is no way to know which ATS programs can collect both the graphic representation of the bullet, as well as the text following the bullet.

It can be very tempting to include a specialized bullet as a branding statement or as a way to differentiate your resume visually. Most word processors allow for diamond-shaped buttons, scrollwork which represents a leaf, color-coordinated square boxes, the checkmark box, the arrowhead, and the French inspired fleur-de-lis.

However, if your target company has an ATS which cannot interpret these special word processing gifts of graphic creativity; they will not be calling you.

Why?

Because the content does not load into the ATS. At best your information is corrupted and shows up as a mish-mash of non-alphabetic characters.

These little gems of personal expression for bullets are coded as special characters or as graphic elements (pictures basically).

The problem?

The ATS is coded (programmed or designed) to accept *text-based* characters and the software does one of two-things:

- Blows the graphic element away and any associated text
  Or
- It loads the graphic element

In the first case, the software will repeat this process until it finds text *not preceded* by a fancy-bullet (graphic element).

Net-net: the resume inside the ATS might have the company names and job-titles loaded but it will not have your experience statements because of this issue with graphic elements used as bullets.

In the second case the graphic element takes up all the available storage space and the text associated with it is blown away to the bit-bucket.

Net-net: the resume might have "wing-dings" characters here and there but it will not have your experience statements.

In both instances – we assumed you messed up the resume. We move on to the next candidate. *This is probably the major reason resumes end up in the digital-black hole.*

While simple dots, dashes and fonts seem boring, they do not corrupt your resume content. Keep it simple!

**Margins**

Another LCD criteria is to use 1-inch margins on every page of your resume. Seriously, use 1-inch margins on every side:

- Top
- Bottom
- Left
- Right

Why are 1-inch margins important?

One-inch margins make the resume:

- Look better
- Easier to read
- Conform to the LCD

In paper form if we layout ten resumes on the same type of paper, regardless of format or layout, guess which one is picked up first? The resume with 1-inch margins.

Why?

It is easiest to read.

Using 1-inch margins shortens the eye-scan travel across the page as well. This makes your content look better in comparison to the competitor who uses smaller margins for the sake of saving a page on a resume. Who wants to read a line of text nearly 8-inches across? You? Your future boss? The recruiter? Nobody!

Not enough of a reason for you? Let us review the LCD aspects.

Do you know what the technology does to your resume? Do you know how the resume is stored, retrieved, or displayed? We cannot possibly know. Which means we play it safe and go with the technical hack of 1-inch margins.

Why?

Believe it or not, some job boards cut off your content horizontally and vertically if larger than their display window. To the recruiter this appears to be a problem with the resume. We move on to the next candidate to be *safe*. "Poof"! Your resume

is auto-rejected.

You do not want to be the candidate who lost out on a job

because you could not bring yourself to use 1-inch margins.

**Ragged Right (AKA: Left Justified)**

When it comes to resume layouts you want to take advantage

of how the eye processes text. For resume reading and review

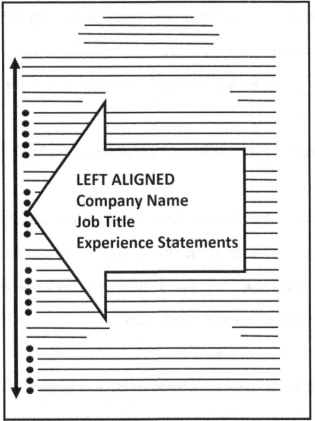

it is best to *left-align* the majority of your content after the intro paragraph. This creates a nice straight edge for the eye to focus.

In the graphic labeled "*Left Aligned*," you can see paragraphs, bullets, company names, and job titles aligned on the left edge. This strategy is designed to control the eye-movement to our advantage. This tactic will likely draw the eye down along the white space between the bullet and the first word of the experience statement.

If the first word of the experience statement is of interest to the hiring manager or recruiter the eye will likely see (if not read) at least 2 to 3 more words via peripheral vision. These 2 to 3 words collectively may allow them to find the necessary context of the statement.

If the first word is not of interest, they can rapidly move to the next experience statement with the least amount of eye-movement or strain.

While this is a people related hack it is more of an autonomic reflex (a mostly unconscious action) by the eye as it processes text. This is technically a bodily-organ hack of the eye. Either way we want to take full advantage (PS: thanks for letting me nerd-out here).

## The Inverted "L" - Typical Eye Scan Pattern

In the graphic labeled *"Typical Eye Scan Pattern,"* you can see the inverted "L" pattern most people follow reviewing a resume. This is not a perfect representation, but typically the top paragraph will be read start to finish if certain rules are followed about length (see Paragraph section). Then the reader will

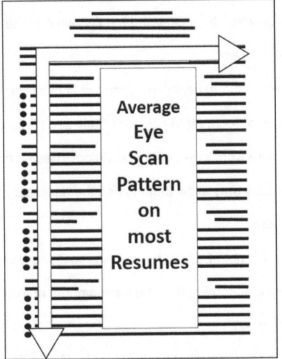

travel down the left side of the resume. The eye tends to focus on the white space between the paragraph bullet and the first word or two of the experience statement (if left-justified) until the reader reaches the end of the page.

## Where the Most Relevant Data Should Be Placed on the Resume

In the graphic "*Most Relevant Data Least Relevant Data*", you can see the resume graphic is divided-vertically in half. As the human reader skims a resume the eye-movement

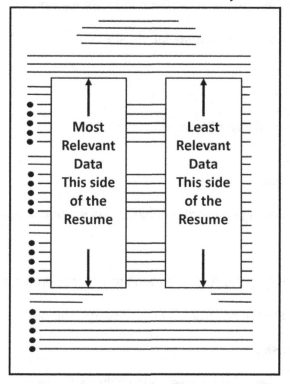

pattern tends to travel down the left side of the resume. We want to take advantage of this behavior by placing the strongest content within the left-vertical half.

Conversely, the least important data should be on the right vertical-half of the resume. This is another eye or vision-processing hack. We can use this insight to arrange and enhance resume content development.

**Section Labels**

In most resumes there are section breaks. These are labels used to help the reader know what they are viewing.

Some common section break labels are:

- Preview
- Summary
- Overview
- Professional Experience
- Career Experience
- Training
- Conferences

Now, the following keyword technique has some risk associated with it.

The algorithms in the ATS programs may not appreciate an attempt to "stuff" keywords into your resume without a context (that is the risk).

But you can "test it" for a week and calibrate the results and change it back, right?

The technique is simple: add your job title as a prefix to the label. In my case that changes section breaks to look like this:

- Recruiter Preview
- Recruiter Summary
- Recruiter Overview

- Recruiter Professional Experience
- Recruiter Career Experience
- Recruiter Training
- Recruiter Conferences

People ask all the time "What is the difference between professional experience and career experience?"

My reply? "Six letters."

There is nothing magical about adding section break labels. Be consistent however you label your content.

Adding job titles (or other keywords) to the section labels is a weak-hack at best. Do more than this lone tactic on your resume. Think of these section Labels as glorified place holders.

Here are more examples of ways to leverage a job title on additional section labels in any resume:

- Recruiter Software
- Recruiter Methods
- Recruiter Tools
- Recruiter Associations
- Recruiter Awards
- Recruiter Conferences

**White Space and Resumes**

We need "white space" in the resume! The trick is to use it correctly. This is another eye-movement or vision processing LCD.

You should put blank lines between logical changes in content.

The graphic labeled *"Blank Line Eye Scan Pattern,"* you can

see right-pointing black arrows which show where blank lines

can be inserted.

The blank line appears above the section header or label and

above each company name in the employment or experience

section (except for the most recent employer which comes first

and is placed directly under the section label). There is *no*

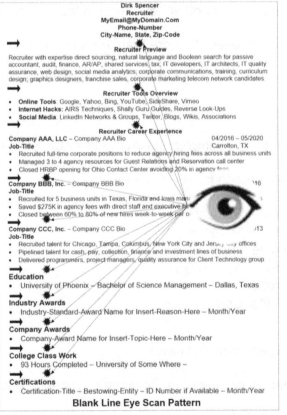

**Blank Line Eye Scan Pattern**

*blank lines underneath the remaining section headers on*

*purpose.*

With this layout, the reader is likely to stop and read the section headers or labels and at least start to skim or scan the experience statement beneath it.

*Without a blank line under the label, the reader will move to the first word of the experience statement immediately beneath it.* Their peripheral vision will passively view the second and maybe the third word on the line as well!

If any of those words are of interest to the reader, they will continue to skim the rest of the document deliberately seeking out their preferred experience bias or the keywords matching the company's needs.

If we added blank lines under the section headers, which seems logical (and most resume templates and designers push this).

The problem?

The reader is likely to move to the next blank line instead of the experience statement. Blank lines are easier for the eye to scan. The eye will fixate on the first available blank-line and re-position to the next blank line, one after another. This is the worst thing to happen on a resume.

Why?

Because the reader will *rationalize* (or believe in their heart of hearts) they physically read the resume when they have skipped the text in favor of blank lines.

They will *feel* they have read the resume (when they have not). They will decide you are not qualified because they saw nothing relevant.

This is one of those people and process break-down points. Even after you explain this to other recruiters or the hiring manager they rarely rehabilitate or change their original opinion. They call this behavior *confirmation bias* (you can Google® it). People do not like to admit they made a mistake like this one. They typically reaffirm their original decision by default. Or they may spend a fair amount intellectual energy to nit-pick the resume to disqualify the candidate. In some cases, to the exclusion of real and relevant experience. Not good.

**Text Style**

Your resume is not the place to showcase your word processing skills. Simply because you know how to add a page border, create a table of contents, or insert a JPEG (Gif, PNG and other image) does not mean you should.

Most resumes are viewed electronically these days.

Why?

Email!

The resume will be handled by the technology:

- Email
- ATS
- VMS
- Job Board
- Social Media Site

We can blame email because it is probably the most used mechanism for sharing resumes with hiring managers. We email people directly. We email them through the ATS. We send email through the VMS if we have one.

Secondly, many companies are penny conscious and discourage printing of emails to save paper and printer costs. Lastly, conservation goes corporate. Companies have *green-initiatives* which further discourage resume-printing.

Naturally, back when resumes were *physically* mailed the company clerk, secretary, and admin assistant and maybe some hiring managers would open envelopes. This meant they would physically see and handle the resumes first hand.

It would be natural for them to gravitate toward fancier layouts, special typography and high rag-count papers.

But we do not handle or view resumes physically much today.

Plus, a paper resume with hand-written notes can become a risk to a company as *discovery evidence* in lawsuits.

Collectively these issues push the paper resume out of vogue in most office settings.

All of this means you want your resume easy to read electronically.

The bigger point? Save those *boss-word processing skills* for your website or portfolio and keep the resume clean and streamlined.

Here is a quick formatting checklist:

- Use the same font-type throughout
- Use the same point-size throughout
- Use the same bullet-type throughout
- Use the same indention-scheme throughout
- Use the same location for section headers or labels throughout

**Who Gives a Font**

Arial has fast become the Internet font standard for commercial websites.

Why?

Because it is easier to read on virtually all types of monitors.

Here I wanted to insert a long discussion on pixels and LED display specs… but I can see your eyes glazing-over from here.

What is the *non-nerd* version then?

Arial works well because it lacks the serif. The serif can be a vertical or horizontal decorative line added to the font to embellish its basic form.

Monitor resolution impact on-screen readability of text the same way it can effect images. Things like pixel rates, aspect ratios, LED, backlighting, and high definition effect how easily text is comprehended.

The lack of a serif (i.e., sans-serif font types) releases a few extra pixels per character. This improves the line pixilation. This means the text looks *crisper and cleaner*. It makes the text much easier to read, speed-read or skim.

Once you pick a font, stick to it everywhere in the resume. Mixing different font types and different font styles can make your content look disorganized.

Next select a point size and use it throughout the entire document.

My best recommendation is an Arial font at an 11-point size. This combination is easier to read than most any other option available.

### The Sin of Random Bolding

Some resume writers think random bolding of keywords will capture the reader's attention.

The truth is eye-movement patterns show the eye jumping from word to word to word. They *do not* read the bolded text.

Instead the eye focuses on the whitespace above the bolded text without word comprehension.

Play it safe and stop random bolding of text.

### The Sin of All Capital Letters

The graphic designer in all of us will drift toward using all capital letters for things like our name, section headers, company names, and the job titles we have held. The problem is all caps is grammatically incorrect. In addition, anyone who's written a text message or email knows all capital letters suggests shouting at your reader. Furthermore, it does not make for a pleasant reading experience. It strains the ocular muscles unnecessarily.

With what we know about eye-movement patterns avoid using all capital letters in the resume.

Essentially use upper and lowercase letters for section labels, company names, and job titles.

## The Sin of Underlining

The underline is a misapplied tool on the resume. Many think it helps the reader when it does not.

In the case of the underline the eye will gravitate to the easiest thing to view or follow.  Which means it will travel horizontally along the white space between the bottom of the word and above the underline. The net outcome is limited to zero comprehension of the words which had the underline applied. Crazy, right?!

Again, it is best to not use the underline feature in your resume.

## The Sin of Italics

And, because your word processor has the feature to italicize words does not mean you should use it in a resume. Italicized text pushes the eye away or off the words you are trying to emphasize. This reduces reader comprehension as well.


## Jargon

Many resume writers and hiring managers will tell you to avoid technical jargon in your resume.

However, if your industry or job-function has its own language and a longer than average history – jargon is your new best friend.

These examples are aimed at people in sales because there is an anthropology or an evolution of terms and practices which can be dated. Showing how your experience has evolved with time-appropriate keywords is a great way to give the hiring authorities confidence in your ability to do the job or adapt.

Sales jargon to include:

- Business Development
- Account Management
- B2B
- B2C
- Inside
- Outside
- Goal
- Quota
- Close
- Metric
- Sold
- Sell
- Sales
- Value
- Partnership
- Relationship
- Consultant
- Spin
- Strategy
- Solution
- Challenger

There is certain jargon and phrases hiring managers are expecting out of your resume by industry. Find out what those words are by reviewing both seminal works and currently published titles. This will allow you to sell yourself as someone who actually keeps up with the industry.

The sales jargon listed above includes a mix of sales methodologies and terms every salesperson should use in the resume.

As a recruiter, our industry jargon is rather unique and bares sharing. Terms to include:

- Cold calling
- Reverse lookups
- Billboard/newspaper ads
- Bulletin boards/company websites
- Job boards/niche boards
- Search engines
- Social media
- Online communities
- News media

You can see from the two examples there are not many words listed when compared to the overall length of average resume. The key is to use the appropriate and current jargon in an effort to make all of your experience appear relevant.

**Where to Find Jargon**

Review these options for developing a list of "hot" terms in your industry:

1. Current white papers in your industry
2. Industry speakers
3. Professional associations

4. Seminal books or periodicals
5. Current bestselling books
6. Professional glossaries
7. Synonyms

**Words Which Blunt Your Impact**

Avoid using these words:

- Other
- Every
- All
- Any

These words are vague. They fail to communicate any degree of scale, value or specificity. Using them will only reduce your value or diminish the scale of your expertise.

Candidates use these words in an attempt to imply a larger context or scale of experience. However, without specifics or examples it does not work. It leaves the reader guessing. The reader will think something comparable to: "Well if you did it all, why not explain some of it here?"

Think about it from their view point. People are pretty frustrated by a lack of clarity on a resume and their frustration is compounded by these kinds of words.

Vague words equal a weak impact on your reader.

**Stop Telegraphing Your YOE**

People share their years of experience (YOE) on a resume in an attempt to convey the depth of expertise or breadth of experience in the industry or job functions.

However, if your number (YOE) does not exactly match the company's number, you have given them a legal opening to remove you from consideration.

How does this work?

Rule number one in this instance - it is all about them.

Rule number two - it is not about you.

Rule number three - no recruiter wants their hiring manager to complain about a resume because it is a mismatch on the years of experience requested.

You might assert: *"But I can add more value with more years of experience. I am willing to take a lower paycheck because I have been out of work too long?* Right?

Compare your thoughts to what the hiring manager is thinking:

*"If I hire this person who has 10 years of experience for a five-year job, he or she will ultimately be unable to perform to their potential. They will become bored. They will underperform in the long run. Also I have to consider when the market turns*

*around and they leave for more money."* These are fear-based rationales or risk-based justifications by both parties. And the hiring manager wins the argument. It is their job opening to manage the way they want to manage it.

**Never Use Humor on a Resume**

A well-qualified candidate, at the perfect price point, with a great personality, and solid business references was not selected because they used the following line on the resume:

*"Head Bottle Washer and CEO"*

This candidate was aiming to convey they had a "can-do" attitude. They wanted to convey how they were not afraid of getting their hands dirty by doing any type of work. It was a metaphor, right?

But the phrase rubbed the account manager the wrong way. We did not make an offer to this candidate.

The resume is a two-dimensional medium. This means the content needs to be related to your skills and not metaphors about those skills. If nothing else avoid humor or sarcasm at all costs.

## TMI Alert

There is some resume advice which recommends sharing personal information. The idea of doing this is it may form a personal connection which leads to a job offer.

This advice must come from a very old source. It must pre-date professional HR implementation and resume technology. And while true for in-person networking it is considered bad form to use this tactic on the resume. There is no context for it or it is usually the wrong context.

Here some examples of TMI included on real-life resumes *not* to emulate:

- *Happily married with three beautiful kids*
- *Wife's name is Mary*
- *Born crafter*
- *Harley lover*
- *Black belt in (insert your favorite or least favorite martial art here)*

True story. Whether it was *Karate* or *Judo*, it does not matter. But the phrase "black belt" stood out on a resume sourced for a customer.

It seemed to me the black belt reference sounded innocent. It was a random piece of data on the last page of their resume. This candidate was professional on the phone and had his career path mapped out.

The candidate was submitted and it seemed like a win-win for all parties.

Unfortunately, the gatekeeper for the client took issue with the black belt information. Their thought, again fear-based (a bias) was the potential risk of violence. The assertion was a person with this background might be prone to hurt people. The candidate might lash out if things did not go his way during a meeting was their parting comment as the phone conversation ended.

True story. This was their position. Their thinking did not consider any of the positives associated with organized martial arts or earning a black-belt.

This can bite you, too. Avoid it by not going into non-work related experiences on the resume. The anecdotes you read about hobby "contacts" hiring someone for work does happen. But it happens in the context of *networking* with *lots of people.* Networking with people is the fastest route to a job – bar none. But sharing your personal interest on a resume will not produce the same outcome.

Depending on their previous experiences, legal strategy, and their rejection criteria this will be a fear-based decision tree. Not hope.

In this case, *black belt* translated to *"violent outburst."* What was the client thinking? The short version went like this: *"Java programmer with a black belt assaults employee's"* news at 11. The company is sued and found liable because it would *reasonable* to foresee how a *trained killer* could be dangerous in the work place. This is an example of how a general hiring bias can affect interviews.

Your best bet? Keep the personal information off the resume unless it is directly related to your experience, industry or specific skill.

## TMI - Vulnerability

Vulnerability statements are a variation of regular TMI disclosures. The difference is these statements offer *highly personalized* information. This form of TMI *immediately* alters the reader's perception of the candidate and negates their qualifications.

Some real-life examples my hiring managers had an adverse reaction to include:

- *"Self-taught"*
- *"Recent death in the family forced me to start my own company."*

The *"Self-taught"* results in the hiring manager deciding the candidate might not be a team player or might not work well with others when learning new processes or systems. While the candidate was attempting to showcase initiative, the hiring manager thought less of it. At a minimum, the hiring manager felt being part of a group and working with others was more essential than initiative? Maybe? We never really know.

The *"recent death"* comment came off as very creepy to the hiring manager. The candidate was aiming for open and honest but failed. Again, people are going to use fear-based decision trees in a pinch.

The candidate wanted to communicate the decision to *"start my own company"* was forced on them by an external event. Secondly, the candidate had hoped to convey his genuine interest in being an employee once again. Either way, digging around this particular example, this one statement made the whole resume feel incongruent.

**Sales Manger versus Sales Manager**

Spell check works *great* when it sees words which are spelled correctly, even the word *manger.* Read that again – *manger.*

The question or debate goes: "Do we forgive the *manger* spelling mistake or is it too risky? Is it an indicator of performance short-comings?"

The consensus on one side goes: "*If the candidate missed manger for manager, what else might they miss?*"

The other side says: "*Everybody makes mistakes, nobody's perfect, we should get that corrected and submit the candidate.*"

From a technical standpoint, recruiters know *there is no correlation between the resume's correctness and a candidate's job performance. Absolutely none.*

But, it does not hurt to reread the resume and as a last quality-check – search for *manger (and replace it)* to be safe.

**Avoid Negativity**

The old adage "*If you cannot say something nice, do not say anything at all*" holds true for resumes, too.

Even in modern resumes some candidates try to describe how bad a situation was when they arrived to a new position. They want the reader to have an appreciation for how bad a situation or project was when they arrived. They feel it is necessary to showcase how they turned things around.

We call these kinds of candidates "turn around kings." They can see where the wheels came off and fix it in their sleep. They command a higher than average dollar amount on salary, too. The challenge is negative words stand out when a resume is scanned or skimmed by the human reader. The intended context can be missed for a dropped word or phrase given how people speed-read the resume. Ultimately, the negative language becomes associated with the *candidate* and not the situation they inherited and turned-around.

Avoid using words like:

- Demoralized
- Depressed
- Discouraged
- Disheartened
- Subpar

Instead write about the actual outcomes on the resume not the conditions inherited. Save those war-stories for the interview and *only* if asked.

### The Kiss of Death

The phrase "The Kiss of Death" did not survive a few rounds of editing but it is back because it is important to realize *how bad* these words or phrases can be. There have been cases where 1-word, a single word caused a resume to remain ranked negatively; below the zero-line.

Vague words lead to vague language. Vague language leads to vague resume content.

Gone are the days when you could throw a bunch of adverbs and adjectives together to "sell" your experience.

Gone are the days when you could throw a bunch of technical keywords or a string of certification acronym candy in a paragraph and land an interview.

Why? The Internet is the great equalizer!

In as little as an hour a recruiter or the hiring manager can deconstruct the foreign language of project management, supply chain, accounting, graphic design, and nuclear propulsion to know what to look for in their resume database (ATS / VMS / Job Board / LinkedIn) and identify the "Doers and Shakers" from the "Blowhards and Fakers."

What makes content vague:

- A lack of granularity
- A lack of specificity
- It raises questions about the content
- It cannot be evaluated easily
- Comparisons are difficult to make

Words in the "fluff" family negatively ranks the resume in the majority of technology offerings. Fluffy-language is no-longer a harmless resume ailment. Why? Because one fluff-word can negatively rank your resume. True story: working with a person who was doing everything right on the resume. They had one fluff-word on page 2 of the resume. Just one. Their resume ranking was below zero.

Fluff words includes hyperbolic language, the use of hyperbole, typical marketing hype; these types of words are your number one enemy to higher resume ranking.

Kiss of Death content includes:

- Obscure terms
- Over-Used terms
- Words prone to misuse
- Phrases which distort experience

The following words and phrases qualify for "The Kiss of Death" list and *should be replaced at all costs*. The technology can destroy the resume's ranking if present:

- Can work independently
- Decisive
- Detailed oriented
- Duties
- Dynamic
- Effectively
- Enthusiastic
- Excellent written and verbal communication skills

- Extensive experience
- Good communicator
- Good listener
- Hands-on Technician
- Hard worker
- High-Energy
- I
- Open door mentor
- Power / Powerful
- Proactive
- Problem solver
- Proven Leader
- Responsible / Responsibility
- Results-Oriented
- Results-Driven
- Seasoned Professional
- Strong
- Strong Interpersonal Skills
- Succeeded
- Successful
- Successfully
- Team Player
- Thinker (all forms: strategic thinker, tactical thinker)
- Utilize (all forms: Utilized, Utilizing)
- Works well under pressure

## Technical Considerations

### No Graphic Lines

The use of graphic lines is a popular temptation inside a

resume. They are easy to add and they appear to organize the

text for the reader. While this was a likely outcome in the days

of physically handling an envelope and paper-resume for

circulation or filing; it is not the case with electronic resume handling. Given the technology used to collect and distribute resumes within organizations, graphic lines can actually cause your data to not be captured inside the ATS.

Technically speaking, the graphic line can appear as a picture file to the ATS. Most ATS programs are unable to properly capture graphic items. This typically means the resume with a graphic line will be rejected entirely or, possibly accepted, but because of the graphics, the text is lost.

## No Page Borders

Another resume graphic in some of the original word processing software was the page border. A page border is placed in the document margins. In the days of paper resumes, this may have helped the document stand out amongst a stack of other resumes lacking page borders.

But today, many of the applicant trackers will see the page border as a graphic JPEG. The net result will be your text is not saved to the ATS.

The recruiters and hiring managers have no way of knowing the empty resume file was due to a corrupting graphic element. They will likely assume it was *user-error* and move on to the next candidate.

## No Text Boxes

Text boxes are not your friend in a resume. This is an instance where the data is physically visible on screen but logically not collected inside the ATS.

Text boxes may be the biggest source of confusion with recruiters tracking candidate profiles in the applicant tracker. The scenario is pretty basic. The recruiter has your resume on screen and calls you based on the information he or she is looking at. What is not obvious at this moment is whether or not your contact information is part of the regular text in the resume or part of a text box.

The conversation closes with something to the effect: "*Call me in a day,*" or "*Call me in a week*" or "*Call me in 10 days*" to review."

Then the recruiter closes the call with: "*I should have feedback on your submission then.*" Boom. Done.

Time passes and you call the recruiter per his or her instructions from the last call or email. You are on the phone with them and while you are talking, you realize they are struggling to find you in the applicant tracker or their spreadsheet.

If your contact information (name, email, phone number) was in a text box, there is a near 100% chance those details did not translate into a physical allocation in the database (ATS).

## No Headers or Footers

Header and footer locations are not places for your contact information either for the same reason. Some ATS do not read the header or footer for information; hence it is not collected.

## No Resume Templates

While many resume templates are available for your word processor – do not use them. Far too many waste valuable space in an effort to control content using the available column "table" technology which may make the content un-readable by the technology.

## The Recruiter Spreadsheets

The Recruiter Spreadsheets are the back-up system used by most recruiters and probably many hiring managers. When companies change technology or if the reporting aspect are lacking the spreadsheets come out. This is where some recruiters live to remain effective during times of technical change.

If you make your contact information *spreadsheet friendly* it is likely it makes its way to the "recruiter" spreadsheet.

Why do you care?

Recruiters share their spreadsheets with each other all the time. While this is a small percentage play my recommendation is to give them what they want, the way they want and become part of this activity.

## Common Mistakes to Avoid

## Resume Job Titles

Resume job titles should be easy to understand and as generic as possible. Recruiters use keywords, and in most cases they start with a generic or industry standard job-title. If the company officially called you "Talent Acquisition Specialist" but you were a *recruiter,* use recruiter on the resume instead. You can always place the official job title to the right of the generic job title parenthetically.

Here is a sample list of easy to understand job titles:

- Recruiter
- Project Manager
- Electrical Engineer
- Product Manager
- SW Engineer
- Software Engineer

- Developer
- SW Developer
- Software Developer

You should focus on job titles with functional skills to maximize their value as a keyword.

No one has ever requested a search on these job titles. If you use any of these on your resume replace them ASAP:

- Entrepreneur
- Owner
- Consultant
- Operator
- Franchisee
- Principal

Yes, we see these words on job descriptions all the time, but we never search using them. Instead consider job titles where they represent the money making, the sales, or the people management aspects of the job. Make it relatable to *their* needs to avoid being auto-rejected.

**Names in Resumes**

Be sure to include your name on your resume. As simple as this sounds, most recruiters will receive at least one or two resumes per month without a name.

The name on your resume should be the name people know you from work. If people know you as "Bob" then use Bob on the resume.

Many candidates fail to receive the follow-up call or email because they used their full legal name, like "Robert David Williams," on the resume, but the email and voice messages references "Bob" or "PJ" or their spouses name.

The recruiter or hiring manager fails to make the connection back to *you* because their reference point is *Robert David Williams*.

The other failure with names on resumes is the inclusion of commas, punctuation, and acronyms. These additional items can turn your last name into electronic dust inside the applicant tracking software. This is an ATS glitch no-one addresses.

**Example – Name with Initial**: Doug V. Smyth

In the example above, the initial "V" and the "." (The period) can become your new last name inside the ATS.

**Example – Middle Name Spelled Out:** Doug Victor Smyth

In this example, the middle name "Victor" can become your new last name. This makes searching by name very difficult.

**Example – Name and Acronyms:** Doug Victor Smyth, PMP, ACIR, MBA

Several things can go wrong with a name formatted like the example above. Either the commas or the added length to the name created by the acronyms can cause the name field to be *blank*.

### Email, Phone Number, ZIP Code

Being reachable is very important once a resume has been submitted. Resumes often lack contact information.

Recruiters open emails too frequently to find a great resume without a phone number or email. How is that possible? People submitting their resume via 3rd party job boards. Sometimes it is actually in some obscure spot on the resume or some font-color which blends into a background color. For a great, one-of-a-kind candidate, we are likely to research the contact information online. But this is a rare occurrence.

In recruiting, expediency will drive the process. This means a better-qualified candidate may be sacrificed for the candidate who is easier or faster to contact if speed to hire is critical. Some hiring managers are okay with "good enough" if time is against them or their projects.

## Bad Email Names

Before becoming a recruiter, some very senior level recruiters told me a bad email name could hurt a candidate's chances for an interview. This seemed like a stupid reason to exclude an otherwise well-qualified individual for a job. The idea of what constitutes a *bad email-name* is relatively subjective too, right? Fast-forward a few years from this information and poof my new profession is recruiting at an agency.

Agency recruiting is a lot of time-to-market or speed-to-market driven behavior. In an agency setting you have to have resumes and candidates ready at a moment's notice. We forward them to the account manager and the account manager forwards them to his customer. That is the agency process.

We had the opportunity to fill an administrative assistant position for a very large company. Landing this position could help the company generate more business over the long haul. As luck would have it, my first candidate prescreen was with an individual who had everything we wanted: good telephone voice, a pleasant demeanor, experience to the correct scale, an empty nester who could focus on her new executive 24/7, and at the exact price point we needed.

Having completed the phone screen, collected the application and copies of the driver's license for the background check and the interview scheduled; the candidate was submitted to the account manager, who was also the owner of the company. He reviewed the candidate's information and within two seconds, he said, "*Find me somebody else. HarleyChick@<domain>.com? We can't take a chance that her email could possibly offend the customer. Good work, but no to this one.*"

My suggestion was to have the candidate create a new email account! Simple. Easy to do, right? Have her pick a generic email, something with her name in it, and update the application, update the resume, and forward the new package to the hiring manager. No harm, no foul.

The owner had a comeback at the ready: "*That's not a bad idea, but what if in a year the candidate slips up, emails something from home over the weekend using her original email, and the customer is offended? What then?*"

The "*what then*" question gave me that sinking-feeling you get on roller-coasters. Her choice of emails made the risk unacceptable. This was the first time I understood how sensitive the recruiting process was for clients and candidates both over email naming conventions. My mentors were correct in their email teachings.

**Email Errors to Avoid**

Beyond the potential salaciousness of an email name, the following errors should be avoided at all cost:

- Missing letters
- Transposed numbers
- Transposed letters
- Wrong domain name
- Missing domain name
- Old work emails
- Old personal emails

**Phone Numbers**

At least once or twice a week someone has listed their phone number on the resume which is incorrect or worse omitted entirely.

As with email addresses, phone numbers are subject to transposed numbers, the wrong exchange, the wrong extension, or the listing of an old cell phone number, former employer or the listing of a... dare I say it a *landline*.

Bottom line - test the phone number using the resume as your reference material instead of re-dial.

**Do Not Forget! It is all about the ZIP Code**

Recruiters typically do an intake meeting with the hiring manager to determine the requirements for their current job posting. This intake meeting subsequently drives the keyword collection process.

Included in the intake meeting is the location of the position. And typically the search will start with the location information then the keywords. Most ATS databases, job boards, and social media sites allow for a location designated by the ZIP Code.

**Where Are You Located?**

On the resume, you should include your city, state, and ZIP Code. You do this for the recruiter and the hiring manager not for the job board or social media site. Most job boards and social media sites collect your ZIP Code information as part of their member sign-in process. It helps them organize their database because they sell their services by location and provide geographical statistics as well.

But by including your city, state, and *Zip Code* on the resume the reader has a direct visual on where you are located. This can break ties between equally qualified candidates!

## Top of the Resume

Start with your name.

Underneath your name list your job title.

Underneath the job title give your email address.

Beneath your email list your phone number.

Below your email under your phone number list the city, state, the ZIP Code together on one line.

You want your contact information in the body of the word-processing document.

Do not place your contact details in either the header or the footer.

Center the information at the top of the page. This is easier on the eyes and makes it easier to copy into other documents.

Lastly, copy and paste your information into a spreadsheet to ensure it appears normal.

Your information should look similar to this:

Your-Name-Here
Your-Job-Title-Here
Your-Email-Here
Your-Phone-Number-Here
Your-City, Your-State, Your-Zip-Code

**List College, Education, Continuing Ed, and Training Separately**

Listing colleges separately from education, separate from continuing education, separate from training is really important because of hiring manager bias.

True story: one of my hiring managers rejected a candidate because they listed their college degrees and continuing education courses under the section header: "*College*".

This was an SMU graduate, a very thoughtful, kind young man working on his career.

The hiring manager was an SMU alumnus as well.

Seemed this would qualify as a warm introduction and probably an offer. Unfortunately, the hiring manager was highly offended by how the candidate lumped continuing education hours for a conference he had attended along with his SMU degree.

The hiring manager was somewhat annoyed and eventually explained his rational by phone. His position was simple; Continuing education hours and conference programs were not akin to a college degree.

In the hiring manager's mind listing these items together was a significant lapse in judgement by the candidate and ultimately someone he would not hire.

Moral of the story?

Keep college separate in its own section. Have a section for conferences only. Have a section for awards only. Have a section for webinars only and repeat this strategy with all of your content. Play the odds. Follow the LCD to minimize these types of manager bias.

It might seem silly. But the value in being this granular with your resume content is invaluable:

1. Maximize keyword content
2. It allows the reader to find *their* hot-topic easier
3. Reduces the risk of reader error regarding content
4. Content appears more organized for limited effort
5. It is easier for the reader to find their bias

## Create a Master Resume

Now what do you do with all this content? Some people think it wise to keep everything you have *ever* done in one huge Master Resume. This *master* would contain all of the information about every one of your job experiences.

For some, this master document allows them to curate their career content. For others it is a way to stay organized during the job search process.

The value of a master resume containing all of your experience is it can be customized for each job submission rather quickly. If this strategy appeals to you, I recommend doing it. Save it somewhere easily retrievable. As you change jobs, gain more experience on the current job or remember an old experience, you use the master resume file to capture the update. Think of it as a diary for your career.

**Using Your Master Resume**

Once the master is completed and saved, you should create file-folders on your computer by target-company. Copy and paste the master resume into each folder. Rename the file in the new folder. The recommendation is to use your name and the word "*resume*" separated by dashes so the eye can readily see it (e.g. Bob Smyth – Resume).

You will use this *copy* of the master resume to create a unique resume for each company submission.

You do this by removing all experiences not directly related to the job you are applying! It is that simple. At this point you have created a customized resume. Do this for each company submission. This leaves the master intact in its original destination.

Do not be afraid to ask for help with this if it sounds too foreign or you do not trust your copy and paste skills.

## What If I Do Not Want a Huge Master Resume?

Okay, looking at my *master* resume one can appreciate not wanting to manage a monstrosity of experiences across several submissions. It is huge. It looks overwhelming.

The option then is to decide to have a single version of the resume which is focused on a specific job-type. Another reason to have a single version of the resumes is your experience is very specific without much variance between companies.

Regardless – let us assume you want to write one version of the resume to manage, then what?

You can do this and be successful with interviews and job offers.

But what if this single-version of the resume is still too large to manage, then what?

Then you must decide how you wish to delineate or exclude experience deliberately. You may have to do this to make the

85

resume easier to view and inviting to read. You need to organize the content around a common strategy. When you have to make such reductions consider one of the following points of view:

- Duration of experience by position
- Proximity to your entry or exit to the position
- Project assignment while in a position
- Complexity of the work

### Duration of Experience by Position

You might select this criterion because the experience being shared constituted the majority of your time with each company. This experience would most likely be the bulk of your effort at each company. This experience would be gained across your elapsed tenure with each firm. This would make obtaining examples, evidence and testimonials about your selectively easier.

### Proximity to Your Entry or Exit to the Position

You select this tactic because it might be the easiest experience to recall and document. It would likely be a select, niche experience which has value to your target position. Recent experience would be relatively easy to document while past experiences could be slightly more difficult to document or recreate for a resume.

## Project Assignment While in a Position

You select this criterion for the same reason you might select duration. But in this case, the project was more significant than the day-to-day operations associated with your job.

## Complexity of the Work

You select this criterion because the complexity or sophistication of the work aligns with your target company. Things to consider include new regulations where there are no existing experts. Technology or service which are new and leading-edge would be potential topical material.

Yes, in all of these examples, things can overlap and generically you could silo your resume content by business unit expertise.

The goal is to give you a structured approach to making decisions about the organization and content being redacted. The goal is not to limit or exclude the wrong content.

And yes, you can pick and choose different criteria for each job listed on your resume! But take the extra minute to keep notes about your decision. This will make interviewing smoother and resume editing easier.

In my case, the idea of showcasing my telecom experience seemed like a good idea in the beginning. But then a friend tells me she could not see herself recruiting for IT people. Brilliant insight for her. This inspired me to revisit my thinking about keeping telecom on my resume. I decided to omit it moving forward. Net result: a lot less information to track. In my case I was never really comfortable reading the industry cycles. Telecom can be a beast in good times! Not enough hours in the day to reach everyone who has to be touched. It can also be a bear in bad times. That was my rational and it is off my resume.

You can make these sorts of decisions for your resume as well. This allows me to focus on audit, accounting, finance, tax and IT for PHP, Java, .Net developers and IT architects and IT network expertise. I can hear you now: *that does not sound like much of a focus, Dirk.*

This combination allows me to straddle two broad business channels: the money side and the technology side.

What are the risks? They do not call me for interviews?

Whatever you decide weigh the risks for your situation.

The good news removing experience you are not committed to is it will force you to be very clean and tight with your content. It will force you to re-organize your skills inventory by each section as well. And it will allow you to increase your keyword density; all good things for the resume.

**Context – The Second C**

Context has everything to do with your actual experience. It comes from your experience with specific tasks and demonstrating certain skills in the modern resume. There is no substitute for explaining what you did, how you did it, who you did it with, who you did it for, how it happened, how you managed change, where these events took place, and why decisions were made.

Context around experience is imperative for the human reader. It gives the hiring manager an understanding where you might fit within their organization.

Context is also required for the machine-reader be it the ATS or job board. Certain aspects of context are required for your resume to be ranked positively. The technology used to manage resumes and rank candidates is done with algorithms, fuzzy logic, and artificial intelligence engines which interrogate your content and rank it against the competition.

As a recruiter, we receive resumes for *project manager* without the words *project management in them!?*

Who does this?

People who are not thinking critically about their resumes?

People receive bad resume help?

Whatever it is to exclude a keyword crucial to your industry is criminal. Thinking you can whiz-bang some fluffy-vague statements on their resume and "*Rah, Rah, Sis Boom Bah*" their way to an interview are mistaken. Those days are long gone. Hiring managers will not waste their time looking for work validation.

This frame of mind works in social settings when networking with like-minded professionals. Those gatherings where being likeable and looking the part opens the door to informal interviews all the time. Networking is the fastest route to a new job – bar none.

You can research (Google or Wiki) Six-Degrees of Separation. It is a math-model which suggest we are fewer than 6 introductions to the person we need to know.

The problem with networking for a job is people under-estimate the amount of effort it takes to knock out those introductions. One motivational speaker has suggested we total suck at estimating the amount of effort it takes to complete a task. Or maybe we under estimate what daily distractions cost us in lost time. Another sales speaker suggests it takes at least 10-times the effort to accomplish *a thing (write a book, paint the house, buy a car, go on vacation… land a job).*

Level of effort aside the technology has leveled the playing field allowing *more qualified* candidates to participate for open positions. It has also allowed better qualified candidates to apply, too.

And, with most hiring moved to a technology-based entry-point, you will need a resume eventually. Therefore - be prepared. Realize the days of "faking it 'til you make it" on a resume are over. Come to grips with knowing you can no longer abdicate resume context development and think the resulting content will land an interview. Think of it this way instead: *better content on your resume can beat the better qualified candidate with weaker-content.*

## Keywords

Keywords are vital to a resume for the following reasons:

- They telegraph industry knowledge
- They document career progression
- They can sometimes validate your scale and skill level

Keywords are important (and maybe the most significant reason) is they are used by recruiters and hiring managers to search for candidates and score or rank the resume.

They also use keywords from social media platforms like:

- LinkedIn
- Slide Share
- YouTube

One of the easiest ways to develop keywords is to use your word processor and take advantage of these four features: definitions, synonyms, antonyms, and the thesaurus.

Most word processors will allow you to right-click a word to see a handful of alternate choices. Use these tools to develop a list of keyword options. Keep it posted somewhere obvious to increase your natural ability to transition ideas across multiple descriptions.

Why should you care about having this many options for keywords?

Since you cannot predict a hiring manager's bias, it is wise to leverage as many keywords as possible. This will allow the hiring manager to find keywords they care about to the exclusion of the other words on the page.

This phenomenon of being blind to content we are not interested in is a common and normal vison-processing behavior we want to hack for our benefit.

As humans we block things from our sight all the time. You open a newspaper looking for the sports score or the TV schedule. Once on the page you do not notice or see content unrelated to your current visual mission.

This phenomenon is called saccadic masking, saccadic suppression or visual-field suppression.

Everyone does visual-field suppression to manage excessive visual input. Magicians use the misleading phrase *retention of vision* when explaining visual blocking during sleight of hand vanishes. In previous Resume Psychology (RP) lectures the word *scotoma* had been used as a *metaphoric* explanation of visual eye-blocking on resumes. Having more keywords improves your odds of having the correct word for each hiring opportunity.

## Resume Keyword Hacks

It used to be *enough* to have a paragraph on your resume with keywords listed in it one after another separated by commas. These paragraphs were blatantly labeled "Keyword Paragraph" or "Keyword List"; recruiters refer to them as k*eyword piles.* These groups of keywords allowed unqualified resumes to rank high enough to warrant interviews.

But the backlash was relatively swift because in under 2 years the ATS industry responded.

Why?

No one enjoys lost time filtering through unqualified candidates via very expensive software. Given the costs of the ATS it has to deliver value on resume scoring in one form or another.

The net effect? Technology vendors re-designed better algorithms and semantic search options. This quickly replaced the simpler and older technology of keyword matching and parametric searches. These changes made the keyword pile ineffective.

The good news is candidates can leverage the new technology. How?

The rules of the written language are immutable. Which is to say it is all about the "words" no matter how they become indexed, parsed, coded and scored to rank a resume!

The trick to leveraging keywords in your resume today falls within four broad ideas:

- Location
- Proximity
- Frequency
- Context

**Resume Keyword Hack Number One: Location**

As in real estate, location is king. On a resume if you were to lay a grid pattern over the text, you could say there was an upper versus lower half horizontally. You can also say there was a left and a right vertical half.

In Western cultures, we read left to right. We want to leverage this condition to our advantage. This means placing keywords in as many spaces as possible in the most viewed locations on the resume.

Others suggest dividing the resume into 4 quadrants parsing keywords in each quadrant. This would be a great idea if people read the resume like a tic-tac-toe board, but they do not. You need your keywords to populate everywhere if possible.

**Resume Keyword Hack Number Two: Proximity**

From an English grammar, programming, and linguistic perspective, keywords relevant to a search will-be closer to other keywords of like meaning, similar context or value. Put another way, they will have fewer words between them.

Word proximity is one of these broadly accepted ideas when it comes to ranking resume content, and in some cases web content by search engine algorithms.

The logic behind the idea of word proximity is comprised of 2 concepts:

- Relationship
- Complexity

Words near or nearer each other than those further apart typically indicates a relationship between those words. This relationship likely represents something more complex than the words or phrases which are further apart suggesting no relationship or less value or less complexity of content.

From a search stand-point this is a rather elegant solution to keyword piles, too.

Why?

Well, too many words too close together, essentially side by side by definition constitutes a "list." In some cases, the list is vertical in a column format. In others the list is horizontal in a paragraph format. *Lists are not a representation of complex ideas, skills or experiences.*

Each artificial intelligence, algorithm and semantic search engine scores this differently. But they all score the resume using this concept of proximity; we use this knowledge to our advantage.

**Resume Keyword Hack Number Three: Frequency**

Keywords need to appear often.

The more times a keyword appears on a resume, the more convincing it is to the reader the keyword is relevant to the experiences being shared. The more times a keyword appears in a resume, the more it is likely ranked higher in comparison to other resumes by the software (ATS, Job Board and Social Media Site) with fewer words.

Again, simple... but sophisticated when done in parallel with the other hacks on keywords.

How many keywords does a resume need? In the early Resume Psychology (RP) lectures, the recommendation was 7 keywords per resume. Today, given the changes to resume ranking and scoring the recommendation is a minimum of 21 keywords.

Think about it, 21 keywords!

One of my HR mentors calculated 21 keywords would be roughly 2% of the average sized resume! That is all. Two-percent! You can fix 2% of your resume, right?!

**Resume Keyword Hack Number Four: Context**

Keywords must have a context. If location is king, then context is queen.

As mentioned before, the ATS industry worked quickly to avoid the occurrence of nonqualified candidates (false positives) being pulled up in searches because they had paragraphs full of random keywords.

The solution most vendors decided upon was semantic search; another way of asking the technology to *"establish a meaning and is there a context present".* This is accomplished by operational aspects of the software. There is an algorithm or artificial intelligence engine being used. Stringing together keywords in a fat-paragraph pile no longer works.

The sophistication of this context-sensitive feature is hard to quantify, as none of the vendors share their approach to this problem. However, it is likely they use a dictionary or grammar engine to quantify or flag vague, empty, and ambiguous language. They *probably* also flag specific hyperbolic keywords or phrases identified by their end-user community as *fluff*. And lastly the excessive use of punctuation present on any one line or area of text is likely flagged.

While this solution is less elegant than others (it is like using a sledge hammer to place a pin) it works well. Bottom line, use your keywords in context.

How?

For developers, it is not enough to write "Java programmer with 5 years of experience." There must be a context. They need to write something along the lines of: *"Wrote Java-based applications using open source tools."*

For project managers, it is not enough to write "project manager" and have a keyword pile. They should write something similar to *"Project managed schedule lags to run more task-actions concurrently."*

For administrative assistants, it is not enough to write *"assisted with phone support"*. They should clarify their experience by writing about specifics, too: *"Answered 50 calls on average per day using multiline PBX."*

## The Inefficient Writing Hack

Efficient communication is all well and good in traditional circumstances: news articles, obituaries, emails, or a great novel.

But in a resume, using efficient writing works against your efforts to break out of the infamous black-hole let alone interviewed or hired.

Why?

Because efficient writing reduces the chance of using enough keyword strategies and branding tactics to be competitive.

*In*efficient writing is the resume countermeasure to efficient writing. *In*efficient writing is the ability to reference the same topic matter (knowledge, skill, or ability) from multiple angles and to do so without being *redundant*.

*In*efficient writing allows the candidate to increase the use of keywords in context. This will increase the recruiter's or hiring manager's confidence in your skills. If done properly it should outshine the competition.

With inefficient writing we are taking advantage of the reader's habit to skim, preview, or speed-reading text. This is another vision processing LCD we want to exercise throughout the resume.

**Inefficient Writing Explained**

Inefficient writing may be the most difficult concept to explain in Resume Psychology (RP) because the word *inefficient* has a negative connotation.

But this is not a typo: inefficient writing is your friend when it comes to resume content.

Inefficient writing allows for increased:

- Comprehension
- Keyword application
- Branding of knowledge, skills and abilities

When done correctly, inefficient writing will ease the reader's ocular stress (eye strain) and lead to *intentional* reading of the resume.

**Inefficient Writing Rules**

The rules for inefficient writing are:

- Express a single idea per experience statement
- Avoid compound sentence structures
- Distil complex concepts to their most relevant point

Lastly with inefficient writing you want to distil complex concepts until you have the most fundamental and salient point properly documented. This requires unhurried thought as it will not feel normal to be this disciplined with using fewer words to explain your experience.

If you follow the rules for inefficient writing, you are forced to be a good steward over your career experiences and their expression on the resume. All of the content on your resume must be tightly focused for the job submission at hand. Without this finite-laser-like focus, inefficient writing will not be effective.

Inefficient Writing - One Idea per Line

Writing a resume to have a single idea per line takes discipline in the beginning. But once mastered there is a rhythm to this type of content creation.

With inefficient writing, individual experience statements must contain one idea or one concept only.

**Inefficient Writing – Compound Content**

To avoid compound sentence structures, learn to deconstruct your experience by avoiding the use of the word "and."

By definition "and" suggests at least two ideas are involved. Develop each idea so it can be presented autonomously. If a piece of your experience cannot stand on its own merits consider removing it, re-write it until it can or dig deeper for better granularity.

Also limit the use of punctuation. That does *not* mean you simply remove the punctuation. This requires you to refine your content deliberately to accomplish this feat of word-wizardry. If an experience statement has quite a few more commas, semicolons or parenthesis it is highly likely the statements needs additional parsing. You want highly defined and distilled content.

When distilling content, you are breaking it into specific sub-parts for improved granularity. Think of it as a form of compartmentalization. There are execution themes, functional themes, business unit tasks in your experience. Learn to segregate each into a cleaner, easier to read document.

Though it feels like you are breaking all kinds of rules about "good writing," remember the resume is not a piece of literature. The resume is your career anthropology. It is your expertise laid out for *their* consideration. With more granular content you make it easier for them to find their biases about what makes a great hire, not yours. If you are any good at what you do, it is your duty to convey it effectively in your resume.

Let us deconstruct an example.

### Example - Experience Statement Using Efficient Writing:

- Designed, developed, implemented customer service software solution.

In this example, there are more than a few commas, which is your first clue there is more than one idea being presented in this experience statement.

### Example - Inefficient Writing - Experience Statements Deconstructed:

- Designed customer service software requirements
- Developed customer service software project schedules
- Implemented customer service software solution used in three regional offices

This example illustrates the biggest benefit of using inefficient writing in resumes. These 3 statements allow the reader to focus faster on his or her particular bias for the job.

The hiring manager or recruiter who cares about *design* experience will quickly find it on the resume and is likely to continue reading the entire statement.

The same is true for those interested in *development* or *implementation* experience. This approach allows them to zero in on their bias instead of missing it because it was buried in an efficient statement further down the line.

Yes, inefficient writing *sounds* counter-intuitive. But the goal is to engage the decision maker on *their* terms, leveraging *their* biases to maximize *your* chances at receiving an interview or an offer.

Per the inefficient writing discussion dense, complex sentences work against our goals in Resume Psychology (RP).

The sentence: "Designed, developed, and implemented customer service software solution" is only helpful if *design* is what the hiring manager is focused on.

Why?

Design was the first word. Because resumes are processed visually it is a speed-reading contest for some or a chore for others.

If the sentence remains in this "trifecta" format and the hiring manager bias or need is for "development" or "implementation" experience guess what? They may never see those other words that far down the line in an experience statement. Few hiring managers will force themselves to "read" a resume with content this dense.

To maximize your chances of the hiring manager seeing all you have to offer (related to their needs) you should unpack or deconstruct the "trifecta" format each time it appears in your resume. Give each idea or experience its own line to shine. This will accomplish two things:

1. It will make it easier to speed read the document
2. It will allow the hiring manager to see their bias faster

This strategy allows you to advance the odds in your favor to capture both the machine and human reader's attention.

**Clarity – The Third C**

Clarity is about the quality of your expression. Clarity speaks specifically to your precision in resume presentations. This includes how well readers understand what you are trying to convey.

In terms of the precision of your expression we are talking about a few key items:

- Your experience expression
- Skill progression
- Scale of experience

Collectively the content of a resume must be easy to understand and easy to remember. The psychological goal of the resume is to create enough clarity the reader internalizes your experience and convinces *themselves* you are the right hire. In this fashion your resume is a *propaganda campaign* about your career anthropology.

**Clarity with Scale**

Perhaps one of the biggest challenges in hiring people is to understand or know the scale of their experience based on a resume.

Hiring managers can be gun-shy moving forward with candidates from lesser-known companies. A bad interview or a bad hire can cause managers to require candidates exclusively from the Fortune X-Hundred Lists.

This requirement can make sourcing candidates super-easy for the recruiter because it narrows the candidate pool. But, it will not stop the non-Fortune candidates from applying, and some of those people will be well qualified.

This is where, if done correctly, the resume can create enough momentum to swing an interview for the non-list candidate. To do this, the resume must show a pattern of increasing responsibility and or skill. This is done by writing in a specific fashion with these key principles in mind about your career and resume presentation:

- Easy to measure
- Reasonable to estimate
- Relevant to their needs

Again, it comes down to the money, the people, and the processes in your career.

Clarity is all about scale.

The easiest way to explain the idea of scale in a resume is to consider someone who calls themselves "CEO."

The CEO of a Fortune 1,000 company has a different scale than the CEO of a five-person operation.

Whatever your "scale" happens to be – own it! If you incorporated as an individual, did consulting work on several projects, and were successful in keeping the cash flow going – own it. It will raise your credibility. But realize it will not qualify you to run something 100 or 1,000 times larger.

Be very clear about the type of work you did, the type of people you managed, the types of budgets you dealt with, and the decision-making you did at this scale. Be proud of it.

Do not make the mistake of trying to present your scale at a level beyond its reality. Hiring managers and recruiters see these kinds of things every week. It is annoying and almost dishonest when candidates try to explain how their "CEO" experience as a one-person operation is no different than the Fortune 500 operation. It is a huge difference; avoid being blinded by your personal vision.

**Clarity with People**

You need to share your expertise with leadership and management.

Your experience should include direct and indirect experience with individuals, teams, and department liaisons. Sharing these people interaction skills can improve your chances of being hired.

**Clarity of Processes**

Working with processes is always tricky. One company's processes are another company's lost profit margin. Today's innovation is tomorrow's standard. Learn to align your process experience carefully. This can include research, training, change management, or implementations.

If done correctly clarity tactics can move a candidate with no Fortune 500 company experience to the interview stage.

**Clarity with Terminology**

When using industry-specific terminology, it is important to do so in a way which is not misleading or confusing.

Too often candidates will mix-and-match keywords (language, jargon, terminology) in an effort to improve how the resume is ranked. The rationale is if they include enough keywords in the resume it will improve its ranking against other resumes. These candidates treat their resume as if it was a web page being ranked by Google.

While this idea is not totally wrong, the keywords need a context. If the words creating context happen to be additional keywords – awesome. Otherwise, this strategy can work against resume ranking and confuse the reader. Once you decide on a strategy, test it and be willing to change it if it is not working.

Avoid mistakes by selecting words based on well-established and accepted meanings. When there is a debate over which word to use choice the more precise option. The goal is to always convey the most accurate description of your experience.

## Clarity with Numbers

Know your numbers! This is critical in a hyper-competitive economy. To do this you need to show how your position added value using numbers. Use this list to brainstorm if you are not sure how to develop your numbers:

- What you spent
- What you saved
- What you were able to negotiate
- What revenue you created
- How you obtained budget approval
- Who championed your budget
- Why the money was important
- What impacts the money produced (beyond finishing the project)

## Ways to Estimate Your Numbers

Every piece of resume advice out there makes mention of the use of numbers. Numbers, numbers, numbers. Over and over again people will tell you to use numbers on your resume.

In my experience, most candidates push back and say they do not have the numbers to share. They claim not being near the budget or not having access to the accounting. They claim they do not understand how numbers work. All of which may be 100% true.

But think about it like this: every job has a cost. The company has to pay those costs. In theory the value of your work contributes to the bottom line. In some fashion the company can afford to pay you given your contribution.

For that reason, you must figure out what the numbers are for your resume. You need to develop a sense of how your job plays out as a budget line item. To help you find a baseline create three types of estimates:

- Conservative
- WAG
- SWAG

The trick is to develop a consistent way of doing your estimates which you can explain quickly during an interview if asked (Google the last 2 acronyms if need be - wink).

Other numbers which might be simpler to work with include: how you saved the company money, percentages on budgets recovered or returned, costs or savings on services or products. You can also look at things like total revenue, gross margins, sunk costs, or expenses. You can also discuss budgets, return on investments or ROI, any totals associated with projects or labor. You can also include the gross or the net profit or loss associated with the company or project you supported.

## Ways to Extrapolate Your Numbers

You can look at your sentences and extrapolate certain data based on the few numbers you might have written about. These examples are contrived. But they may allow you to have a better *feel* for how to estimate numbers without misrepresenting the facts.

For example, if you saved the company $100 dollars a week. It would be reasonable to use the $100-dollar amount per week to extrapolate a yearly number. At a $100 dollars a week times 52 weeks you could estimate an annual savings of $5,200.00 a year. If these changes were in place during a 10-year career, the gross savings would be $52,000.00 ($5,200.00 times 10).

The experience statements on your resume might read:

- Saved the company $5,200 dollars annually by reorganizing shop workflow
- Netted $5,200.00 in material costs by eliminating unnecessary process steps
- Reduced costs by $52K over a 10-year period by sourcing new vendors

You can also reduce the length of these statements to their most essential elements and repeat them in a new paragraph. You can use them as a Cost Savings Summary, Money Returned or a Cost Reduction Overview section:

- Reduced shop workflow costs by $5k

- Saved $5K in material costs
- Achieved $52K in process savings

Having numbers on the resume creates another layer of confidence about you because it telegraphs how you are aware of the importance of money to sustain the business. All without saying "*I have excellent business acumen.*"

## Consistency – The Fourth C

There are two forms of consistency related to resumes. Those related to the presentation of your resume on the monitor (print out) and those related to your career experiences. These two items require different skills when preparing the resume.

The book has addressed consistency of layout, font selection, point size, spacing, and positioning of section labels.

The more complex idea of consistency is how you share or relate your career experiences.

In this context consistency comprises job progression, salary increases, and job scope. This requires a deliberate attention to detail and showcasing increased skill acquisition.

## Job Progression

In terms of consistency with career progression, what we are really talking about is job-hopping. Typically, it is not the actual job-hopping which bothers hiring managers and recruiters.

Instead, what bothers hiring managers and recruiters is the subtle, unspoken meaning of the job movement.

It appears as if you had no discipline, resources, or maturity to maintain job stability.

And right now you might be saying, "*But Dirk, I am the victim of a slow economy, and I took any job I could to keep the cash flow coming in.*"

While it is good to demonstrate your willingness to keep working. The truth is we have hiring professionals who read those tea-leaves and have a negative view of your *decision making process.*

Why?

For some to take "any job" suggests you may lack a capacity to plan or anticipate company or industry trends. It can be taken as a negative regarding your decision-making skills.

While not a fair analysis it happens all the time. Be ready to explain the job movement with confidence not embarrassment.

**Salary Increases**

Even if the recruiter explains the "cash flow" job decisions, the hiring manager will not automatically be enlightened or moved by such an explanation. They have a bias toward seeing your salary go-up. You may or may not readily change *those minds*. But if you interview with a manager like this be prepared. Be comfortable when you explain the salary differential. If you were over-paid before – say so. If the segment tanked – be able to prove it with data or an industry trusted reference.

**Job Scope**

You need to be prepared to explain how each job grew your scope of skills. Any job movement made to keep the lights-on needs a *glimmer* of progression.

You want the job activity to collectively make sense by showing a strength to create opportunities and not to be pulled along by happenstance or the economy at-large.

**Remember: It Is about Them!**

The fact is most people in the hiring process have their own biases on which skills and experiences matter most. This can leave a candidate guessing as to what to include in their resume.

So what is the counter-measure to skills or experience bias? *Have experience in the area being advertised!* Second and equally as important the candidate must make their skills and abilities overt, obvious, and aligned to the position at hand. Since you cannot know the specifics of *their needs* ahead of time you need to parse *your experience*. You wish to take full advantage of inefficient writing as an example. Granularity this fine makes it easier for *them* to find *their* definition of needs on your resume.

Candidates assume skills and abilities will get them hired, but this is not the whole picture.

But technically it is your ability to present specifics, enough specifics to generate enough confidence in your skills they become eager to interview or hire you without question.

This is why detailed and granular content wins over the machine and human reader.

There is no way for a candidate to investigate skills bias among target companies.

If a candidate lacks a specific experience, the hiring manager will consider the time and costs to make a candidate productive. Under those conditions most hiring managers are not jumping at the chance to make an offer.

Hiring can be a complicated, convoluted and an extended process.

Of course, there is no way to explain any of this in a job description.

**Avoid Skills Above and Beyond Their Need**

Many resume books and career coaches present the idea of using transferable skills as a means to a job. This is misguided advice for resumes. Transferable skills *should* be exploited in an existing job. It is true people can carve out great careers at companies using transferable skills. *Omit the transferable skills-sales pitch from the resume.*

Candidates are taught to use transferable skills as a way to sell themselves into a job where they lack specific experience. Other advice suggests transferable skills create a higher value to the hiring authority.

But this tactic backfires when used on the resume. Recruiters and hiring managers are looking for something very specific to *their* needs. This creates a certain level of bias toward *their* perceptions. It has nothing to do with *your* thoughts on being an ideal fit, quick study or showcasing transferable skills.

When you present transferable skills on the resume the hiring managers will begin calculating how, why, and when you will leave for another opportunity in the area where you gained your transferable skills. Or they focus exclusively on your transferable skills to the point they quickly disqualify you given all these *unrelated* skills.

No hiring manager, no HR department, and for sure, no recruiter wants their job to be a stepping stone to something bigger down the road. They want to hire candidates who are excited and genuinely interest in the job at hand. They are not really interested in your career aspirations. They are not really interested in your long-range job plans. Avoid this trap by not using the transferable skills pitch in the resume.

Now, if *they suggest* your transferable skills are key to their job; your job is to agree and shut-up. Let them sell this concept to you and themselves without any help. It needs to be their idea 100% of the way.

## Why is Writing Resume Content Difficult?

Unconscious competence may be the largest road-block people encounter when attempting to develop their resume content. How does that happen?

Easy. You do the work. You gain the experience. No one makes you explain how you do it. True?

Over time you execute with less and less conscious effort because you have more and more experience. Eventually you make it look effortless.

Unconscious competence is great for skill-based behaviors. Things like driving a car or driving a project. But it is also probably the reason people are eager to farm out the resume writing process. It can be difficult to get into your own head and dissect experiences.

Decide you are willing to drill down and take a critical look at your experience. Decide it is worth the effort to develop great content so your resume can help you land a job.

Too many people want to farm out the resume writing process to someone else. It is very understandable.

The problem with 3rd party resume content is it does not take long for recruiters and hiring managers to figure out you did not write your content. This is typically because resume writers have a style of writing and canned resume layouts they use over and over for all of their customers.

And it is *not* cheating to use a resume writer. However, the recruiter or the hiring manager will wonder, "*If he/she farmed out the resume, what else might be farmed-out if they get this job*?"

Why do *some* managers think this way?

The news reports of employees using online or remote freelancers to do their job is on the rise.

This can cause some hiring managers to be hyper-sensitive to discovering their candidate used a resume writer. They may draw a corollary which is not logical.

Whether logical or not, fair or not it is another reality in a world where outsourcing is not confined to corporations.

Bite the bullet and be engaged with the writing process to avoid any negative misconception of you.

## A Word Regarding Resume Writers

Having the integrity to say you wrote your own resume is not the only reason to consider not using a "professional" resume writer.

The other consideration is more pragmatic. Most have no experience with the recruiting technology.

While most are college educated and many hold terminal-degrees worthy of admiration they lack exposure to today's resume technology.

Because of technology (job boards, social media, and applicant tracking software) the resume has to speak to the *human reader* and capture the attention of *the machine* at the same time.

Without experience with database development, search heuristics, or applicant tracking software, the average resume writer lacks the technical exposure and therefore cannot readily adapt their expertise to overcome these implications. If you hire one ensure they have the bandwidth to work with you in a collaborative fashion.

**You Care the Most Regarding Your Job Prospects**

Plus, trust me, trust yourself, *no one* is going to care if you land a job or not more than *you*. Period. No one knows your career skill-set and scale better than you either.

Full disclosure – I used a resume writer. It was in a time before home printers and neighborhood copy shops. The cost was a whopping $800 dollars. This netted me a box filled with printed copies of the resume on colored paper. It also included a summary page of my career. It listed things about me which sounded official and important.

The resume writer was a retired journalist who covered a peanut farmer turned governor who later became President and multiple book author Jimmy Carter.

My resume writer was a professional wordsmith with mad-skills. His computer and printer at this time was an all-in-one model called a *typewriter*.

The resume landed me a handful of interviews but no offers. The few interviews I had did not go well because the content felt foreign to me. It was someone else's work product technically.

I had read the resume several times. The content was accurate, but it was not my creation. The factoid-list did little but sooth my ego between interviews. It would make a great checklist for a biography perhaps?

The lesson? The content did not feel real to me. In my case it did not feel authentic. It felt like cheating.

This is not to say you cannot have help writing your resume or have a better experience or a better resume writer. My point –

find all the help you need *and* be actively involved in the content creation aspects.

**Putting It All Together**

Measuring the success of your resume is simple. Are you receiving offers?

Yes or no?

That is it.

In the world of Resume Psychology (RP) we want the hiring authority to read your resume and come away with the simple, solitary and burning thought, *"We should hire this person."*

This thought should play in their mind while doing other things. It should drive them to talk about your expertise with their peers. Their peers will ask to see your resume and they should agree, *"You're right. We should hire this person."*

When you follow RP you should ultimately make the document easier:

- For the recruiter to champion your candidacy
- For a hiring manager to justify an offer
- For HR to expedite the onboarding process off-schedule

People do not mind going the extra mile on your behalf when they understand the value you will bring to their company.

## Resume Content Creation

Candidates need to take control of the resume writing process. The bulk of resume content creation should rest with you and not be abdicated to an outplacement service, certified resume writer, or a well-intended insider with no recruiting experience. You can approach this in several ways:

- Collaboration
- Quality review
- Reference this book

When you collaborate with the resume-writing service you want to engage them in the revision process until you land a job. Be polite while assertive until you have a document which achieves offers.

You can compare the rules in Resume Psychology (RP) with your resume as a quality check. You can follow-up with specific editing requests. Your resume writer does not have to agree with these principles! But they do have to do what you want if their service is designed to land you a job.

## Going It Alone

If you go it alone with your resume, be willing to read the material in this section and mimic the examples. You want to test the resume and measure the feedback you receive. Make adjustments based on the feedback and re-test. Repeat this process until you achieve the results you want.

## Time to Product

Regardless of your situation, applying the Resume Psychology (RP) techniques to an existing resume should take a few focused hours maybe a short-weekend.

## Resume Action Steps

1. Make the changes and corrections
2. Post the resume to a job board
3. Measure the results over a 3-day period
4. Make additional adjustments based on the feedback

## The Three Day Period

The 3-day period should start on Monday, Tuesday, or Wednesday. The worst days to start an online resume test are Friday, Saturday, and Sunday.

## Measuring Outcomes

If you are receiving one or more calls a week, the resume is doing a reasonable job of generating interest. It could be worse, but there is room for improvement. Make structured changes. Evaluate previous changes. Test and re-test the changes.

If you are receiving one or more pre-screen phone calls a week, recruiters are finding the necessary keywords and reviewing your availability. Contact with people is always better because you can exercise your networking muscles.

If you are interviewing with a hiring manager one to two times a month, you have legitimate traction in your industry. Contact with decision-makers is always best.

And remember: unless you receive an offer turn everyone you meet into a networking contact! You never directly ask about the job again.

Instead: stay connected by sharing potential business leads, names of potential hires, industry-trade information. Put this activity on your schedule and work the schedule.

## Resume Psychology Checklist

Here is where you can expedite applying the principles from this book. If you jumped to this section after previewing the material, go back into the book for an explanation on anything you might not understand.

The bottom-line:

- Change it
- Test it
- Check the results
- Change some more
- Repeat until job offer

The following checklists are arranged by topic, not in a chronological fashion. If it is obvious to you what the problem is with your resume – start there first. If it is not immediately obvious dive in where your instincts tell you.

**Content – Resume Layout and Format**

☐ Use a reverse chronological resume if at all possible

☐ Keep Intro paragraph to 3 lines

☐ Use only conventional bullet points

☐ Use left-justified text

☐ Use 1-inch margins on all four sides of the page

☐ Add the job title to section labels (Recruiter Experience, rather than Experience)

☐ Use white-space between logical changes in content

☐ Use the same font-type throughout (Arial)

☐ Use the same point-size throughout (11)

☐ Use the same indention-scheme throughout

☐ Use the same location for section labels throughout

☐ Use inefficient writing (1 idea per line)

☐ Research and include modern jargon

☐ Check your spelling, verb-agreement and hyperbole

☐ Include your correct contact information

- [ ] Use a professional sounding email address

## Content – Stuff to Stop Doing

- [ ] Avoid random bolding

- [ ] Avoid using all caps

- [ ] Avoid underlining

- [ ] Avoid italics

- [ ] Avoid Kiss of Death language

- [ ] Avoid vague language, especially words like *every* and *all*

- [ ] Avoid including *total* YOE (years of experience)

- [ ] Avoid using humor

- [ ] Avoid Too Much Information (TMI)

- [ ] Avoid negativity

- [ ] Do not use graphic lines

- [ ] Do not use page borders

- [ ] Do not use text boxes

## Context – Leveraging Keywords Effectively

- [ ] Research keywords to include

- [ ] Include keywords on the right side of the page

- [ ] Keep keywords close together

- [ ] Repeat keywords often, but be sure the content still sounds good

- ☐ Include 21 keywords
- ☐ Include keywords in sentence context
- ☐ Unpack any "trifecta" sentences

### Clarity – Be Specific

- ☐ Avoid highlighting transferable skills
- ☐ Make sure your resume is in your voice (and not the voice of your resume writer)
- ☐ Own your achievements
- ☐ Be clear and honest about scale
- ☐ Use numbers to quantify success

### Consistency – Be the Same in How You Present

- ☐ Be clear about career progression
- ☐ Be able to explain job-hopping
- ☐ Ensure you are using the same font throughout
- ☐ Double check bullets are the same size everywhere
- ☐ Have the same distance between bullets and the text behind them
- ☐ Use the same indention scheme throughout the resume

## Resume Review

To show you what a resume looks like following the RP rules, one is included below.

It happens to be my resume with some experience left out to save space.

Several of the sections contain real information and others contain placeholder data.

Below the resume samples there will be sections of the resume taken in pieces and reviewed independently.

The goal is to show you how the RP strategies come together.

In many instances I also explain mistakes.

## Sample Resume:

Your-Name-Here
Your-Job-Title-Here
Your-Email-Here
Your-Phone-Number-Here
Your-City, Your-State, Your-Zip-Code

### Recruiter Preview
Recruiter with expertise in direct sourcing, pre-screen and qualifying candidates using job boards, search engines, social media and associations and white-papers for IT, engineering, accounting, finance, graphic design, call-center leadership, compensation and HR Benefits.

## Recruiter Tool Summary

- **ATS**: Infro, PeopleAnswers, Taleo, iCims, JobVite, MaxHire, cBizOne
- **Paid Services**: Monster, DICE, CareerBuilder, Indeed, LinkedIn Recruiter

## Recruiter Sourcing Experience Overview

- **Online Tools**: Google, Yahoo, Bing, YouTube, SideShare, Vimeo
- **Internet Hacks:** Shally Guru Guides, AIRS Techniques, Reverse Look-Ups
- **Social Media**: LinkedIn Networks & Groups, Twitter, Blogs, Wikis, Associations

## Recruiter Career Experience

**Hotel Corporation USA**        01/Year – 12/Year
**Hotel Chain with 500 properties**      Dallas, TX
**Recruiter** (FTE Corporate / Field Recruiting)

- Recruited Juniper Network Operation Center (NOC) experts for telecomm center
- Managed 3 to 4 agency resources for Guest Relations and Guest Reservation call center
- Used area alumni chapter to find Project Managers for application development program
- Sourced Treasury Analyst for bank administration of corporate credit card holders
- Searched HR/Labor/Employment attorneys via state and local bar associations at no cost
- Used LinkedIn to find Cash Flow Capital Spend experts per venture capital model
- Performed X-Ray searches on PDF, PPT, XLS and DOC files to harvest resumes
- Hacked revenue manager names and emails from affinity boards and conference lists
- Leveraged association web sites to mine candidate phone numbers and emails

**Portable Power Corporation**       01/Year – 12/Year
**500 stores** nation-wide         Dallas, TX
**Recruiter** (FTE Corporate Recruiting)

- Saved approximately $240K in agency fees with staff and executive hires
- Closed between 60% to 80% of new hires week-to-week per on-boarding statistics
- Recruited business intelligence SQL Server BI Stack developers for market intelligence
- Recruited SalesForce.Com administrators, architects and developers for market intelligence
- Hired MBA accountant specializing in GL, GAAP and EOY reporting 20% below market
- Used private associations, LinkedIn Recruiter, groups and Slideshare.Net to find talent
- Recruited point of sale engineers, print media buyers, real estate managers
- Worked requisitions for merchandising, sales, real estate, training, metal buying (recycling)

**Big Bank, LLC.**             01/Year – 12/Year
**Bank with offices in 100 countries**      Dallas, TX
**Senior IT Recruiter** (Contract for FTE Hiring)
- Recruited talent for Chicago, Tampa, Columbus, New York City and Jersey City offices
- Pipelined talent for cash, pay, collection, finance and investment lines of business
- Delivered programmers, project managers, quality assurance for Client Technology group
- Managed a requisition load of 20 to 35 openings in Taleo for 7 managers
- Managed LinkedIn Recruiter Dashboard to harvest .Net and JAVA architects
- Used LinkedIn Recruiter Dashboard to source technical and financial project managers
- Sourced in Taleo quality assurance testers and application optimization engineers

**College Degrees Completed**
- <College Name> – Associate of Arts (AA) – Plano, Texas
- <University Name> – Bachelor of Science Management – Dallas, Texas

### Professional Training
- Big Time Conference, <Sponsor Name> – 01/Year
- Big Name Expo, <Sponsor Name> – 02/Year
- Webinars Series, <Speaker Name> – 03/Year

### Continuing Education
- Class Title, Topic or Subject, 3 Credit Hours – 04/Year
- Seminar Name, Topic Name, 5 Credit Hours – 05/Year

### Certifications
- Former Project Management Professional (PMP) Certification (Number 01010101)
- Facilitation Techniques / Teamwork Communication Techniques (IBM)

**[End of Sample Resume]**

### Resume Debrief

Much of this debrief will seem obvious if you have read the book sequential.

My goal is to help you appreciate how to master the editing process for your resume.

This is a section-by-section explanation of the resume. Each will be flagged by the phrase: **"Example - <Resume Area>"** like the one below, so let's started!

### Example – Top of Resume:

Your-Name-Here
Your-Job-Title-Here
Your-Email-Here
Your-Phone-Number-Here
Your-City, Your-State, Your-Zip-Code

**In Detail**:

Center this cluster of text. Doing so will make your resume look balanced. This is the expected layout. We leverage visual processing hacks with the eye and this layout makes it easier for the recruiter to copy and paste you details into other documents, emails, or spreadsheets. Include your name, job title, email, phone number, and city, state and zip code.

**Example - Opening Paragraph:**

**Recruiter Preview**

Recruiter with expertise in direct sourcing, pre-screen and qualifying candidates using job boards, search engines, social media and associations and white-papers for IT, engineering, accounting, finance, graphic design, call-center leadership, compensation and HR Benefits.

**In Detail:**

- **Recruiter Preview.** Every logical section in the resume should have a "label" to help orient the reader. The paragraph label should include a keyword or job title acting as a keyword when possible. You can do this to all section labels where appropriate.

- **Recruiter with expertise in…** The start of the sentence contains the job title, which is also a keyword. If the ATS highlights keywords having one at the start of the paragraph is highly beneficial. The phrase *"with expertise"* is recommended for 2 reasons: One, it presupposes you as an expert. Two it shows confidence in your experience. This might be enough social proof to generate an interview request all on its own. It may trigger an impulse call to pre-screen you.

- **...direct sourcing, pre-screen and qualifying candidates...** This portion of the paragraph contains three skills. These skills happen to be keywords in my industry. The only wasted word is "and." If the reader is not interested in these three skills, it means 1) I have applied to the wrong type of recruiting job, or 2) I am using the wrong terminology for the job.

- **...using...** This is my transition word in the paragraph. The word(s) you select for the transition will be context driven.

- **...job boards, search engines, social media...** This is a series of key-phrases. The individual words in the phrases are technically keywords, too. Bonus! Honestly, this is a happy accident, but you want to create as many of these happy accidents on your resume when you can. These keywords are about tools used in my industry. If the decision-maker is not interested in these tools, we have to hope *they* see and then sell themselves on transferable skills. They have to sell this to themselves though. In the case of different job boards is probably not an issue. But if they have a full-blow VMS instead, they may move on to candidates with more of that experience instead. Selling my personal info at the end of the resume (crafting, origami) will not be a tie-breaker.

- **…and associations and white-papers…** This text telegraphs additional search skills in non-conventional places. Technically, these are not keywords or phrases. Using these examples represents a risk. What if the reader does not know about these resources? What if they had limited or no success with these resources? My personal experience has been positive. In my mind the *risk* is acceptable. I would prefer to work somewhere open to new ideas or working with people who already do this on the job. If not it is probably a bad fit all around.

- **…IT, engineering …accounting, finance…** Again we are flirting with a lot of keywords and not about skills. These are the industries, departments, or business units I have previously sourced for. If you follow this example, select the ones where you have the most relevant experience.

**Example - Summary of Tools:**

**Recruiter Tool Summary**

- **ATS**: Infro, PeopleAnswers, Taleo, iCims, JobVite, MaxHire, cBizOne
- **Paid Services**: Monster, DICE, CareerBuilder, Indeed, LinkedIn Recruiter

**In Detail:**

- **ATS...** Technically, using an acronym in this case is the better way to go over the phrase *Applicant Tracking System*. ATS is a key acronym in our industry. The *micro-mistake* that could get me rejected would be if I wrote *ATS System* somewhere in the document. The word *system* is redundant. This can be a pet-peeve for someone in the hiring process. It could be an opportunity to coach me. There is no way to know. With the colon behind the acronym we make it a label for the line itself.

- **...Infro, PeopleAnswers, Taleo, iCims, JobVite, MaxHire, cBizOne...** These are all ATS vendor names. It is a great example of how keywords are all around you. Check on your previous vendors or vendors of the competition. The micro-insight here would be to list not only the vendor *tools* but also vendor *names*. In this example PeopleAnswers was acquired by Infor. Infor has a ton of tools from Cloud services to a full blown CRM. Could these small things be a tie-breaker? Only slightly, but we want to take every reasonable edge we can.

- **Paid Services**: This is a word phrase made into a label using the colon. The words *Paid Services* are not a true keyword for the recruiting piece of the job. Technically is a vague or generic word which carriers a positive impact. The phrase may telegraph awareness of costs and indicate a comfort level with managing paid-services. This is an attempt to show an awareness of costs without using the word. It could make my *non-paid* skills stand out where the company lacks recruiting budget. Lots of ways to slice my content... learn to do this with your information.

- **...Monster, DICE, CareerBuilder, Indeed, LinkedIn Recruiter...** You guessed it, more tools. Are they keywords? Who cares! We do! Monster is the tool. There company name is TMP. TMP usually runs large scale automated recruiting and social media campaigns for firms who can afford a total turn-key solution. CareerBuilder is

owned by 3 media companies TEGNA Inc., Tribune Media

and The McClatchy Company. Two of these firms are

traded on the NY Stock Exchange. Including the vendor

names where I had experience working with them directly

might play better for some decision makers.


**Example – Recruiter Career Experience Section:**

### Recruiter Career Experience

**Hotel Corporation USA**            01/Year – 12/Year
**Hotel Chain with 500 properties**      Dallas, TX
**Recruiter** (FTE Corporate / Field Recruiting)

- Recruited Juniper Network Operation Center (NOC) experts for telecomm center
- Managed 3 to 4 agency resources for Guest Relations and Guest Reservation call center
- Used area alumni chapter to find Project Managers for application development program
- Sourced Treasury Analyst for bank administration of corporate credit card holders
- Searched HR/Labor/Employment attorneys via state and local bar associations at no cost
- Used LinkedIn to find Cash Flow Capital Spend experts per venture capital model
- Performed X-Ray searches on PDF, PPT, XLS and DOC files to harvest resumes
- Hacked revenue manager names and emails from affinity boards and conference lists
- Leveraged association web sites to mine candidate phone numbers and emails

**In Detail:**

Include the company name, employment time frame, job title, and location for each relevant work experience. Follow this section heading (and others) with an experience statement (or related section heading content) *and NOT a blank-line.*

- **Recruited...** In the first experience statement, the first word is a keyword when possible. Alternately, use a strong action verb (that is redundant actually but you never know who is reading these things, Dirk).

- **...Juniper Network Operation Center (NOC) experts...** These are industry keywords. They are the evidence of another work segment. Using both the keyword and the acronym will help the recruiter find my experience by either option. The keyword and the acronym will be repeated together if possible for the one-two punch it allows in recruiter searches.

- **...telecom center...** This is another key phrase about the industry. It provides a context to support the search activity mentioned. We might be able to live *without* the word "center." But with it, it *"compounds"* the experience of the keyword Telecomm. *Compounding keywords* is a difficult "tactic" to execute well and will be part of a separate chapter book or blog.

**Example – College Section:**

**College Degrees Completed**
- <College name> – Associate of Arts (AA) – Plano, Texas
- <University Name> – Bachelor of Science Management – Dallas, Texas

**In Detail:**

As in other examples, we have a label above some bulleted text. Be accurate here. Make it easy to know if your degree is complete or in progress.

The bulleted text contains simple, direct and easy to understand details. Spell out your degree *and* use standard abbreviations. In my example, the abbreviation for my bachelor's degree is not standard so it is spelled with no acronym.

**Example – Training Section:**

**Professional Training**
- Big Time Conference, <Sponsor Name> – 01/Year
- Big Name Expo, <Sponsor Name> – 02/Year
- Webinars Series, <Speaker Name> – 03/Year

**In Detail:**

As in previous examples, this part of the resume needs a

section label. Given what you now know about bias, keep each

experience separate and differentiated from your college

degree(s). You can use an alternate label. In my case, it could

be "Recruiter Training" as a label.

The bulleted text contains the title, sponsor (potential keyword),

and speaker details. Be smart and use the content with the best

keywords or skills important to your industry. The experience is

dated to show relevance. I would exclude training where the

content has changed due to time.

**Example - Continuing Education:**

**Continuing Education**
- Class Title, Topic, or Subject, 3 Credit Hours – 04/Year
- Seminar Name, Topic Name, 5 Credit Hours – 05/Year

**In Detail:**

Continuing education, for some hiring managers, proves you

are passionate about the career, office skills or technology.

The bulleted text shows a recommended layout. Sharing the

credit hours cleanly and simply validates the material. Again,

dates show how recently you pursued this professional

development.

**Example – Certification Section:**

**Certifications**
- Former Project Management Professional (PMP) Certification (Number 01010101)
- Facilitation Techniques / Teamwork Communication Techniques (IBM)

**In Detail:**

The label here is Certifications. Again, adding the job title to the label (Recruiter Certifications in my case); if true, would be worth doing. Show certifications related to the job you are applying exclusively.

**[End of Resume Debrief]**

**In Conclusion**

The predictions of a new *"thing"* replacing resumes has not come to pass. Why? It is likely the money. Companies do not spend budget dollars on recruiting processes, people and technology unless absolutely necessary.

In view of this you *will continue to need* a modern resume written with these goals in mind:

- Beat the machine: Leverage the LCD and the 4-C's
- Be seen: Leverage inefficient writing and keywords
- Get hired: With a laser-focused resume for *each* submission

It takes effort and you can do it!

## Thank You!

Thank you for reading this book. Your support is an exceptional gift to *any* writer. My hope is you found this book an easy and informative read.

Best regards,

Dirk Spencer

Creator Resume Psychology

Author *Resume Psychology: Resume Hacks & Traps Revealed, Beat the Machine, Be Seen & Get Hired!*

## Appendix A: RP Frequently Asked Questions

### 1. How many keywords should I have on my resume?

The magic number appears to be at least twenty-one keywords on a resume. Do not include keywords from your section labels in this count. Twenty-one keywords make up less than 5% of the total word count in the average 3-page resume.

### 2. How many pages should my resume be?

Two pages is a safe bet, assuming there is a 3$^{rd}$-page containing information about education, awards, certification, training, patents, authorship, and speaking experience. If the 3$^{rd}$ page is 30% (or more) additional work experience, be sure it is highly relevant and well-written.

### 3. Do I need my street address on the resume?

No. The street address is immaterial to the way recruiters segment candidate pools using zip code based searches.

### 4. Should I include my personality profile results in the resume?

No. Things like personality or aptitude test outcomes rarely enhance your perceived market value or work experience. Unless these documents are specifically mentioned in the job description, or you have source evidence the company uses such data for interviews, it is not recommended for the resume.

### 5. I was told to put education on the first page since I am a teacher. Why?

Teacher hiring is predicated on degree completion in order to become certified or licensed in most states.

**6. What do I do about companies that have gone out-of-business or merged with other companies?**

List their names, as they were when you worked for them. These are sometimes classified as "legacy" company names. If the company went out of business, only share this news if asked. No need to volunteer a sad story if no one is interested.

If the company has a new name, list the new name to the right of the old name in parentheses. This can increase your keyword hit rate. Here are some examples from real-life:
- Perot Systems (Currently Dell)
- Dell (Previously Perot Systems)
- EDS (Merged with HP)
- EDS (Now an HP Company)
- HP (Formerly EDS)
- HP (EDS Ex-Pat)

**7. What can I do about gaps in employment?**

Not a lot. Own them. You have to have a ready answer for the pre-screen or interview. Rehearse a simple, 10 to 15-word explanation about the gaps. The answer should be brief, easy to understand and true.

With gaps, recruiters and hiring managers will worry about things like a medical emergency, family tragedy, pregnancy, or incarceration (jail, prison, mental) but they are not allowed to ask. Be forthright with the information so they worry less.

**8. Do I include personal hobbies on the resume?**

No. The only exceptions are if 1) If the hobby relates to the job specifically, or 2) you made and maintained personal contact with the hiring manager within the context of the hobby.

9.  **What is the best job title to use if I was an entrepreneur in my last job?**

My recommendation is the job title should be the function or duty being done for the skills being required by the job. Do not get sucked into the trap of selling yourself as a *jack-of-all-trades* or through your *transferable skills*. Instead, be the manager, salesman, or technical lead. Anything job title beats the word entrepreneur, owner, or CEO for a one-person consulting company.

10. **Why do you recommend "the brightest white" paper I can afford for paper resumes?**

Bright white paper simply looks cleaner, neater, and crisper. It also stands out much better than you realize. You can easily test this out at your local copy center.

11. **What's the difference between a resume and a curriculum vita?**

Technically the resume is a document sharing your career or job experience. In comparison, the American Curriculum Vitae or CV has its roots in academia and the medical profession. It is designed to showcase educational credentials and specific medical expertise. Outside the US, the terms are less interchangeable and are subject to differing cultural standards.

12. **Should I include my volunteer or charitable experience on my resume?**

Only if the target company sponsors the organization where you volunteer or sponsors the charity in an open and public fashion.

### 13. What's the worst resume mistake ever?

It is the one hurting your chances at a job right now.

Seriously, it is a matter of degrees. If the only thing wrong with your resume is it is missing a phone number or email, then it is the worst mistake ever. If you fail to use current terminology because you think your industry has not changed, then *that* is the worst mistake ever. Misspelling the company name is a huge no-go for most hiring managers.

### 14. Should I customize my resume for each ATS?

This is a nice idea, but it is why I developed the LCD rule. Vendors offer multiple versions of their product at the same time and do not publish technical papers on these differences.

### 15. Is there a way to know which ATS the company is using?

Yes, usually it is listed in the web address of the employment portal or automated responses sent via email. You can use this information to verify if an agency has legitimate access to your company or not.

### 16. Why does the LCD sound made-up?

Because it is. I developed it as a way to coalesce the most common attributes of the recruiting process and technology when developing resume tactics and strategies to work across most if not all platforms.

### 17. What is the best way to get my resume to the target company?

Follow their online advertised process as closely as possible. After, it would be reasonable to mail or deliver a physical copy of the resume. It should include a note stating you have applied online and wanted to demonstrate your continued interest.

### 18. What is the best way to reach you?

Assuming this not the year 2525, you can find my contact details on SlideShare.net and LinkedIn.com.

### 19. What is the best source for keywords in my industry?

Typically, vendors supporting your industry will have the best, and potentially the most current keywords to draw from. The specifications for their services, products, or tools will be keyword rich. If the vendor is a certification prep provider, find out when they performed their last course audit, or when the course was last updated to avoid out of date practices and jargon.

### 20. I have been in the same industry 20 years. Why would I update my terminology?

Sharing how your experience has adapted with the passing of time is a great way to prove your skills are relevant without having to say it aloud.

### 21. Do agencies or staffing firms have a standard resume layout I can use?

Some agencies use a template and if you are working with one which does, you will be offered an example to follow. If they have a template, it is an attempt to provide their clients with a uniformed presentation. For others, it is a branding tool so their connections can find *their* candidates over the competition.

## 22. Why are there this many different recommendations on resume layouts?

Recruiting is a very competitive business with very thin margins. The agencies want their candidates to stand out over their competition. Having a company-sponsored format is one way to differentiate with their clients. This is especially true if they are competing with multiple vendors through a VMS.

## 23. What if my recruiter wants to change my resume?

If the recruiter is submitting your resume to their client, leverage this insight. Do this for their submission only and track the resume's progress.

## 24. Are there any tools to measure if you have enough keywords on your resume?

Doing a manual word count should be sufficient. As mentioned before, twenty-one keywords would be a minimum to have.

## 25. Is it Applicant Tracking System or Applicant Tracking Software?

ATS can mean either one. The take away is each company takes a different approach to their ATS.

## 26. I read a story where this company did away with resumes. Is that going to become a trend?

Probably not. Go on their web page and apply for a position. You will likely get a quick quiz about your experience which will feel like a replay of a resume; go prepared.

**27. What happened when you created fake profiles to test your ideas?**

Many of the companies never knew the profiles were a test. They would call, ask for the persona posted and I would take a message. As things became busier, I would tell them their person had taken another offer. The companies who did find out were not amused.

**28. What should I do if my resume writer will not help incorporate your suggestions unless I pay them more money?**

The book was designed so you could modify your resume section by section on your own. If you have the budget, find another resume writer locally, show them what you want done and gain their commitment before you pay. If you are out of budget, then make a game night project out of fixing your resume. Have a handful of friends divide and conquer your resume content section by section using the checklists and samples in the book.

**29. What if a "master" resume is too much for me to keep organized?**

This is covered in detail in the book. The short answer here – you can have one version of the resume focused on one set of skills. Having a master resume is a way for people to be better curators of their experience when it is varied.

**30. How do I land a job in an area where I have no direct experience?**

This is tough. It requires serious networking skills to find opportunities where you lack the experience. If this is your situation Review my online presentation: *Networking on Purpose* located at *www.SlideShare.Net/DirkSpencer.*

There are several versions of this presentation available. I used conference speakers as targets. You can substitute potential hiring managers and recruiters at your target-companies instead.

## 31. How do I prepare for interviews with or without a resume?

My suggestion combines the idea of rehearsing your information aloud with time-spaced reviews of your answers. This is where you build honest and genuine confidence about your interview answers. This is very different from memorization. If you need insights to this concept find my Interview Psychology presentation at www.SlideShare.Net/DirkSpencer.

## 32. What if I have no experience for the job I am targeting?

Do more networking with way people in that space! It will take 10-times the level of effort than you think to land your next job in this situation. Hiring managers, recruiters and HR professionals reference *qualifying experience* for their open jobs for a reason. My SlideShare.Net page will have a presentation on this topic soon.

## 33. You do not mention SEO or Search Engine Optimization, why?

SEO or Search Engine Optimization does not directly apply to resume content because of the LCD of the ATS technology.

## 34. Do you provide resume writing services?
No. I believe strongly people need to own their own content about their experience. I provide resume coaching and social media strategy on a fee-bases if we are a match for working together.

## Appendix B: References

1. A Pocket Style Manual by Diana Hacker
2. American Optometric Association (AOA) Database
3. American Psychological Association (APA) Database
4. An Introduction to Human Communication: Understanding and Sharing by Judy C. Pearson and Paul E. Nelson
5. Applied Science Labs (ASL) Citation List (Eye Fixation)
6. Arrington Research (Customized Search Engine)
7. Association for Computing Machinery (ACM) Digital Library
8. Barron's Business Dictionary Series: of *Finance and Investment* Terms by John Downes and Jordan Goodman; of *Business and Economics* Terms by Jack P. Friedman Ph.D. C.P.A; of *Insurance* Terms by Harvey W. Rubin Ph.D.; of *Accounting* Terms by Jae K. Shim Ph.D. and Joel G. Siegel Ph.D.; of *Computer and Internet* Terms by Douglas Downing Ph.D. and Michael Covington Ph.D.; of *Finance and Investment* Terms by John Downes and Jordan Elliot Goodman; of *Real Estate* Terms by Jack P. Friedman Ph.D. and Jack C. Harris Ph.D.; of *Banking* Terms by Thomas P. Fitch; of *Marketing* Terms by Jane Imber and Betsy-Ann Toffler; of *International Investment* Terms by Jae K. Shim Ph.D. and Joel G. Siegel Ph.D. CPA; of *Mathematics* Terms by Douglas Downing; of *Tax* Terms by Larry Crumbley and Jack Friedman
9. Black's Law Dictionary (Multiple Editions) by Bryan A. Garner
10. Copyediting and Proofreading for Dummies by Suzanne Gilad
11. Design Elements Typography Fundamentals A Graphic Style Manual For Understanding How Typography Affects Design by Baker and Taylor
12. EBSCO Database Effective Study by Francis Pleasant Robinson
13. Effective Study by Francis Pleasant Robinson
14. Evelyn Wood Reading Dynamics by Evelyn Wood
15. Gartner Magic Quadrant for Enterprise Search Report 2013
16. How to Increase Your Sales at No Cost by Robert D. Clark
17. How to Make People Like You in 90 Seconds or Less by Nicholas Boothman

18. How to Say It: Choice Words, Phrases, Sentences, and Paragraphs for Every Situation by Rosalie Maggio
19. Human Communication in Society by Jess K. Alberts, Thomas K. Nakayama
20. IScan Inc. (Eye Telemetry)
21. Jeffrey Gitomer's Series: Little Black Book of Connections 6.5 Assets for Networking Your Way to Rich Relationships; Little Platinum Book of Cha-Ching! 32.5 strategies to ring your own (cash) register of business; Little Red Book of Sales Answers: 99.5 real world answers that make sense, make sales, and MAKE Money; Little Teal Book of Trust: How to earn it, grow it, and keep it to become a Trusted Advisor; Little Red Book of Selling: 12.5 Principles of Sales Greatness by Jeffrey Gitomer (with Jessica McDougall on select titles)
22. Magic Without Apparatus by Camille Gaultier
23. Manual of style for use of copy editors, proof readers, operators, and compositors engaged in the production of executive, congressional, and departmental publications by United States. Government Printing Office
24. McGraw-Hill's Proofreading Handbook 2nd Edition by Laura Anderson (Author)
25. Modern Coin Magic by J. B. Bobo
26. Now You See It, Now You Don't by Bill Tarr
27. Perfect Phrases Series by Ken O'Quinn
28. Photo Reading: by Paul R. Scheele
29. Phrases That Sell: The Ultimate Phrase Finder to Help You Promote Your Products, Services, and Ideas by Edward Werz and Sally Germain
30. Psychology: An Introduction by Jan by Charles G. Morris and Albert A. Maisto
31. Psychology by Richard O. Straub and David G. Myers
32. Psychology Today (Periodical / Archive)
33. Essentials of Human Communication by Joseph A. Devito
34. Retention Vanish by David Roth
35. Scientific American (Multiple Editions)
36. Senso Motoric Instruments (SMI) (Neuroscience feedback via the eye)
37. Speed Reading by Tony Buzan
38. Start & Run a Copywriting Business by Steve Slaunwhite

39. Take Charge of Your Mind: Core Skills to Enhance Your Performance, Well-Being, and Integrity at Work by Paul Hannam and John Selby
40. The Art of Writing Advertising: Conversations with Masters of the Craft: David Ogilvy, William Bernbach, by Denis Higgins
41. The Associated Press Stylebook by Associated Press
42. The Chicago Manual of Style by Chicago Editorial Staff
43. The Complete Manual of Typography: A Guide to Setting Perfect Type by James Felici and Frank Romano
44. The Copywriter's Handbook: A Step-By-Step Guide To Writing Copy That Sells by Robert W. Bly
45. The Elements of Style, Fourth Edition by William Strunk Jr., E. B. White
46. The Gentle Art of Verbal Self-Defense by Suzette Haden Elgin
47. The Media of Mass Communication by John Vivian
48. The Merriam-Webster (Multiple Formats) by Merriam-Webster
49. The New York Times Manual of Style and Usage: The Official Style Guide Used by the Writers and Editors by Allan M. Siegal and William G. Connolly
50. The Oxford Essential Guide to Writing by Thomas S. Kane
51. The Pocket Ad Writer by Ernie Blood
52. TMP World Wide Archives
53. Tobii Technology Archive (Gaze Point)
54. What to Say When You Talk to Yourself by Shad Helmstetter
55. Writing Copy for Dummies Jonathan Kranz
56. Advanced Certified Internet Recruiter (ACIR) (Blog, Wiki, White-Hat Hacking)
57. http://api.careerbuilder.com/ResumeInfo.aspx (Resume API Code)
58. http://booleanblackbelt.com by Glen Cathy (Semantic Search, ATS, Boolean)
59. http://booleanstrings.com by Irina Shamaeva (Boolean, Search Engine Sourcing)
60. http://taxonomy.sla.org (Taxonomy Organization)
61. http://www.dice.com/common/content/util/apidoc/jobsearch.html (API Sample)
62. http://www.hedden-information.com/index.htm (Controlled Vocabulary Search)

63. http://www.programmableweb.com (How to use APIs)
64. http://www.quora.com (Search Science News / API Issues)
65. http://www.smartlogic.com (Taxonomy & Ontology Vendor)
66. http://www.synaptica.com (Ontology / Taxonomy Vendor)
67. https://business.linkedin.com/talent-solutions/partners (API ATS Partners)
68. https://dev.twitter.com/rest/public/search (Search developed)
69. https://moz.com/ (Internet Article, WWW White-Paper and curated list Sourcing)
70. https://www.searchenginenews.com (Search Engine News)
71. People Sourcing Certification Program (Boolean, Google, LinkedIn Sourcing)
72. SearchEngineLand.Com (Search Engine News)
73. SearchEngineNews.Com (Search Engine News)
74. SearchEngineJournal.Com (Search Engine News)
75. SearchEngineWatch.Com (Search Engine News)
76. Source Con Conventions (ERE Media – The Recruiter Training Conference)
77. Sourcing Ninja Social Talent (Ethical Recruiter Hacker Training)
78. The Certified Internet Recruiter (CIR) (Boolean, Natural Language Search)
79. The Sourcing Institute (Boolean, Natural Language, Search Engine Hacking)
80. www.eremedia.com (Recruiting Trends, ATS, Search Strategy, Boolean)
81. www.searchenginejournal.com (Search Engine News)
82. www.searchengineland.com (Search Engine News)
83. www.webopedia.com (Boolean, Sourcing, Ethical Hacking, Search Engine)
84. www.yext.com (Location Based Sourcing)
85. Wiki Pages: Eye-Fixation, Eye-Telemetry, Gaze Points, Gaze Replay, Saccadic Masking, Saccadic Suppression (Visual Blocking), Computational Linguistics, Word Sense Disambiguation, Word Stemming, Polysemy, Classifying Characters, Semantic Search, Search Algorithm, Inverted Index, Proximity Search, File Indexing, Keyword Search, Context & Intent, Machine-Parsing, Ontology, Taxonomies, Metadata, API Keys, Pattern Recognition, Search-Based Software Engineering (SBSE), Metaheuristic/Heuristic Search Methods, Natural Language Processing, Latent

semantic indexing (LSI), Latent semantic analysis (LSA), optimal recognition point (position) (ORP).

**Appendix C: In Memorial**

Dr. Jerri L. Williams (1944 - 2002) Professor of English

A purple-ink wielding Aggie professor who opened my eyes to the science of writing. She submitted my poem written following her process (*A Kennedy Dies*). It received *An Emerging Scholar award in English*. This validated her assertion if you follow the rules you can create a repeatable process for writing *anyone* can follow; even if they have no interest in creating poetry. She was determined to *teach* her students by sharing her hard-won expertise. Those fortunate enough to have attended her classes were better students for it.

Made in the USA
Monee, IL
17 October 2023

# HAVE YOU BEEN TURNED ON TO LIGHT NOVELS YET?

## 86—EIGHTY-SIX, VOL. 1–11

In truth, there is no such thing as a bloodless war. Beyond the fortified walls protecting the eighty-five Republic Sectors lies the "nonexistent" Eighty-Sixth Sector. The young men and women of this forsaken land are branded the Eighty-Six and, stripped of their humanity, pilot "unmanned" weapons into battle...

**Manga adaptation available now!**

## WOLF & PARCHMENT, VOL. 1–6

The young man Col dreams of one day joining the holy clergy and departs on a journey from the bathhouse, Spice and Wolf. Winfiel Kingdom's prince has invited him to help correct the sins of the Church. But as his travels begin, Col discovers in his luggage a young girl with a wolf's ears and tail named Myuri who stowed away for the ride!

**Manga adaptation available now!**

## SOLO LEVELING, VOL. 1–5

E-rank hunter Jinwoo Sung has no money, no talent, and no prospects to speak of—and apparently, no luck, either! When he enters a hidden double dungeon one fateful day, he's abandoned by his party and left to die at the hands of some of the most horrific monsters he's ever encountered.

**Comic adaptation available now!**